The Classical Temper
in Western Europe

The Classical Temper in Western Europe

Papers from the annual symposium of the
Australian Academy of the Humanities

edited by
John Hardy and Andrew McCredie

Melbourne
OXFORD UNIVERSITY PRESS
Oxford   Auckland   NewYork

OXFORD UNIVERSITY PRESS

Oxford London Glasgow New York Toronto
Delhi Bombay Calcutta Madras Karachi
Kuala Lumpur Singapore Hong Kong Tokyo
Nairobi Dar es Salaam Cape Town
Melbourne Auckland
and associates in
Beirut Berlin Ibadan Mexico City Nicosia

National Library of Australia
Cataloguing-in-Publication data:

Australian Academy of the Humanities. Symposium
(13th: 1982: University of Adelaide). .
The classical temper in Western Europe.

Includes bibliographical references and index.
ISBN 0 19 554465 X.

I. Arts, European—Congresses. I. Hardy, J. P.
(John Phillips,) 1933—. II. McCredie, Andrew D.
III. Title. (Series: Symposia (Australian Academy of
the Humanities)).

700'.94

OXFORD is a trademark of Oxford University Press
Designed by Falkenmire Cullen Graphic Design
Typeset by Abb-Typesetting, 81-83 Little Oxford Street, Collingwood
Printed in Hong Kong
Published by Oxford University Press, 7 Bowen Crescent, Melbourne

Contents

Acknowledgements

The papers in this volume were originally presented at the Thirteenth Annual Symposium of the Australian Academy of the Humanities, which was held at the University of Adelaide, 21–23 May 1982. That was the first time the Academy had met in Adelaide, and the first time its Symposium had been widely advertised as open to the general public. The success of the Symposium has ensured that the Academy will follow the practice of inviting the public in future years.

The Academy remains grateful to the South Australian Government through its Department for the Arts, and to the University of Adelaide, its Foundation and Vice-Chancellor, Professor D. R. Stranks, for substantial encouragement and financial support in enabling it to meet in Adelaide. It also wishes to thank the Myer (South Australia) Stores Ltd for making a contribution, the Friends of the Gallery of South Australia for providing free publicity, and Ansett Airlines of Australia, the official carrier for the Symposium, for helping with the organization.

John Hardy
Andrew McCredie

Contributors

Georg Feder, Director of the Joseph Haydn Institute, Cologne

Elliott Forysth, Professor of French, La Trobe University

John Gregory, Lecturer in Visual Arts, Monash University

John Hardy, Professor of English, Australian National University

Colin J. Horne, Emeritus Professor (formerly Professor of English), University of Adelaide

John Steele, Professor of Music, University of Otago, Dunedin

Anthony Stephens, Professor of German, University of Adelaide

P. A. Tomory, Professor of Art History, La Trobe University

Francis West, Professor of History and Government, Deakin University

Introduction

John Hardy

This Symposium follows on the conference held to mark the two-hundred-and-fiftieth anniversary of Joseph Haydn's birth. When Professor Andrew McCredie broached the possibility of the Academy's contributing to this event, it seemed appropriate to choose a theme that would add in some significant way to what was being planned. To that end it was decided that the theme of the Symposium should be classicism, or, more precisely, 'The Classical Temper in Western Europe'. Papers will be devoted to Italy, France, England and Germany as well as Vienna, and focus on literature, painting and history as well as music. The period of most concern to us will be the three hundred years or so from roughly the beginning of the sixteenth to the early nineteenth century, when classical ideas were pervasive in a number of different ways.

The later date seemed to select itself in view of the earlier Haydn conference. The choice of the other terminus needs, perhaps, a word of explanation. Renaissance humanism, which gave expression to man's intellectual and moral nature, and therefore to distinctly human values, had its beginnings two hundred years before the sixteenth century, and its reshaping of the intellectual life of western Europe meant that the medieval tradition became transformed by ancient practice. The beginning of the sixteenth century seems, nevertheless, a suitable starting-point. It was then that so many artists of the Italian High Renaissance utilized ancient examples and made such a distinctive use of space and form. The earlier half of the sixteenth-century was also the major period of neo-Latinity when the reverence for the ancients produced not only conscious imitation but extensive compendia. These aimed at a *copia verborum et rerum*, a 'copiousness of style and subject-matter', and the enduring significance of these collections lay in what they contributed to vernacular writers.

This may provide a hint for our continuing discussion throughout the Symposium: the creative use made of the classical past by those who found it a source of inspiration for their own independent and original works. The trend of recent scholarship has been in this direction. Some years ago, in introducing the proceedings of a Cambridge seminar on 'Classical Influences', Robert Bolgar noted the shift from research 'centred on identifying the Greco-Roman originals' to a recognition of the need 'to establish what elements were generally selected for borrowing, and how it was that the borrowed material proved fruitful'.[1] A Michelangelo or a Bramante, for example, a Pope or a Dr Johnson, might usefully be discussed in this context.

The use of classical material is, however, so widespread and so disparate that one problem is to set relevant bounds to our period. Another is the perennial and more tantalizing problem of definition. What do we mean when we call certain compositions 'classical', or 'neo-classical'? Are we talking about a particular style, or something else? What are the defining characteristics? How important is the sense of tradition? What role should be allowed to creative innovation, to inspiration rather than more formal rules? And if the baroque, say, shows a sense of structural coherence inherited from the classical,[2] how exclusive should any definition be? The art of Greece and Rome was scarcely homogeneous; while the two most famous 'antiques' of the Renaissance were the Apollo Belvedere and the Laocoön. Obviously different artists made use of different models, but did they sometimes view the same models in different ways? Anthony Blunt has noted that there are 'exceptions to the rule that Baroque artists were attracted to Baroque models and classical to classical', and he adds: 'The tastes of Borromini at one end of the scale and Poussin at the other are in general consistent.'[3]

Classicism may well be so protean, so open to different shapes and applications, as to be most profitably regarded as a conveniently adaptable, rather elastic concept; and this not just in terms of its various 'elements', of the different possibilities it seems to offer, but also in terms of the different uses to which it has been put. The ancient world has stood as a cultural ideal; yet in other ways, too, it has been used as a means of authorizing or justifying particular innovations or points of view. Certainly there is a sense in which a classical past, however mythical, has been invoked to provide a model of leadership or government as well as of civilization and the arts. A sense of exclusiveness has been inherent in the term 'classical' from its very beginning, and the use that has been made of this will sometimes interest the historian of ideas or the historiographer, or the social or political historian, as well as the historian of the arts.

If a history of classicism in western Europe since Greek and Roman times were ever to be written, it would be an immense undertaking, extending well beyond our designated period, from at least the Carolingian Renaissance to modern times. It would have to record the relevance of classicism to a vast number of events, movements, and influences: the transmission of manuscripts and the transmission of ideas (not forgetting the readiness with which these could be adapted); the movements of individual scholars and their visits to, say, Italy, as well as national movements and events like the English Restoration, the French Revolution and the reaction to it, or, in Germany, the response of Weimar classicism to the French Revolution and Napoleonic expansion. Besides the general influence of a classically-oriented schooling, history itself would need to be considered as playing a vital role—its modes of apprehension and the temper adopted towards the past; in particular, the way writers saw themselves during, for example, the European Enlightenment as heirs of classical antiquity. And obviously one would need to take account of other things: Pope Leo X's ambitions for the city of Rome, or the excavations at Pompeii and Herculaneum. Often we forget how pervasive the influence of classicism has been, from Wedgwood designs or neo-Palladian architecture to the Virgilian words that still appear on the back of the American dollar bill.

In attempting during this Symposium to sketch certain important chapters in any such history, we shall be primarily concerned with the meaning of classicism for the historian of the arts, the critic of music, painting, and literature. Yet in considering these 'sister arts', does some distinction between them need to be made? Is it, for example, that generalizations can seem to have more relevance for painting rather than literature? Can one take a phrase of Leonardo's out of context and say that painting is capable of a 'simpler completeness' ('facile sattisfatione')[4] than literature or poetry (though, of course, a misunderstanding of the way imagination is present in a literary work limits Leonardo's argument in the 'Paragone')? Even in literature, however, classicism has been associated with an emphasis on the more formal properties of a work, with, as one French literary historian has said, 'an immense effort to establish everywhere an order which is as reasonable as the order of mathematics, to organize a sort of social and aesthetic geometry'.[5]

'Classical' tends to be used with words like 'moment' or 'temper', rather than with words like 'mood' or 'movement', where 'romantic' might nevertheless be appropriate. It would, however, be a mistake to think of the classical as devoid of feeling or movement, or even of a concern with the senses; though used as an aesthetic term it gives, above all, an impression of control and order, of balance and restraint, of an achieved resolution or a peculiar harmony and poise. A 'classical' work is the product of insight rather than impulse, is self-contained rather than open-ended, and is never self-indulgent in its expression of emotion or feeling. Its details, though arguably so finished in themselves, are 'composed' in such a way as to clarify and support one another, adding up to a totality that is harmonized or focused. Perhaps one may say that such a composition achieves, through an inner equilibrium of its component parts or forces, an eloquent kind of impersonality, where the creative artist seems, curiously, both present in and distanced from the completed work.

A 'classical style' was described by James Joyce in his manuscript *Stephen Hero* as 'the syllogism of art, the only legitimate process from one world to another'. For Joyce's Stephen 'the supreme artist' had to 'disentangle the subtle soul of the image from its mesh of defining circumstances most exactly', re-embodying it 'in artistic circumstances chosen as the most exact for its new office'. Joyce also speaks of 'the gropings of a spiritual eye which seeks to adjust its vision to an exact focus', and the 'exactness' is, I take it, that of art, the apprehension of the universal in the individual.[6]

This aspect of the classical has been attested in various ways. Socrates thought 'the sculptor must represent the activities of the soul through form'.[7] Giorgio Vasari, the sixteenth-century historian of Italian Renaissance art, praised Leonardo's figures for their 'correctness, improved order, right measure, perfect drawing, and a godlike grace'.[8] In bringing the Grecian Urn alive in his imagination, Keats described the scene depicted on it as 'all breathing human passion far above'. Often there was a tendency to attribute to the classical something transcendental. Friedrich Schlegel regarded it as an attempt to embody infinite ideas and emotions in a finite form, while earlier Winckelmann had written (and I quote two short passages from Henry Fuseli's translation):

> They [i.e. the Greeks] began to form certain general ideas of beauty, with regard to the proportions of the inferior parts, as well as to the whole frame: these they raised above the reach of mortality, according to the superior model of some ideal nature.
>
> It is not only *Nature* which the votaries of the Greeks find in their works, but still more, something superior to nature; ideal beauties, brain-born images, as *Proclus* says [Proclus was the fifth-century commentator on Plato].[9]

Literary apologists maintained something similar, though with an authority also derived from Aristotle: the greater truth poetry is capable of—what Shelley associated with the 'unchangeable forms of human nature',[10] of which Homer might provide an example. The means of achieving such a comprehensive representation of experience have, however, been variously understood, and especially during the seventeenth and eighteenth centuries, when mathematical rationalism held sway, there was a tendency to look to the so-called 'rules' as providing the most secure or even the only basis for literary excellence. In the words of Pope's *Essay on Criticism*, the 'Rules of old' were 'Nature methodiz'd'. The sophistications of this theory were strongest in seventeenth-century France, and one might take as an example French 'classical' theatre. Yet in the hands of genius the 'rules' could, of course, impart vitality to the form. Nor does the imaginative life of a work need to depend on its adherence to the 'rules', and in English or Weimar classicism or even in France one can discern inherent and creative tensions between the supposedly inherited form and the individual talent.

A corner-stone of the 'rules' was the concept of decorum. Horace's *'quid decet, quid non'* ('what is fitting, what is not') was reinforced by the rhetorical tradition and applied to a multitude of things—from theatrical gesture to poetic landscape, from the necessary relationship between architecture and landscape to the details of linguistic usage, or the elements that went to make up a given literary kind, whether epic or drama, tragedy or comedy. The concept of decorum was infinitely extendable in indicating the importance of propriety in subject-matter and expression; indeed, the French critic René Rapin regarded 'the *decorum*' as 'the most essential' and 'universal' of the rules, to which all the others must, in turn, 'be subject'.[11] It was, however, a concept open to a variety of interpretation. It could be reduced to a mere formula, amounting to a kind of aesthetic traumatropism in the hands of those whom Quintilian might have described as 'a dried-up, withered and bloodless band'[12]; alternatively, it could breathe new life into the conjunction of form and content, becoming, in Milton's words, 'the grand master peece to observe'.[13] Whereas many critics condemned Shakespeare for not observing the distinction between tragedy and comedy, Dr Johnson realized that his plays were 'compositions of a distinct kind', which, in their more varied and comprehensive representations of life, more deeply engage our attention.

One thinks of Shakespeare as a classic of our literature rather than as a classical dramatist, yet an illustration of what I would call his 'classical temper' might be drawn from Johnson's defence of his characterization against the rigid prescriptiveness of his detractors:

> His adherence to general nature has exposed him to the censure of critics, who form their judgments upon narrower principles. Dennis and Rhymer think his Romans not sufficiently Roman; and Voltaire

censures his kings as not completely royal. Dennis is offended, that Menenius, a senator of Rome, should play the buffoon; and Voltaire perhaps thinks decency violated when the Danish usurper is represented as a drunkard. But Shakespeare always makes nature predominate over accident; and if he preserves the essential character, is not very careful of distinctions superinduced and adventitious. His story requires Romans or kings, but he thinks only on men. He knew that Rome, like every other city, had men of all dispositions; and, wanting a buffoon, he went into the senate-house for that which the senate-house would certainly have afforded him. He was inclined to shew an usurper and a murderer not only odious but despicable; he therefore added drunkenness to his other qualities, knowing that kings love wine like other men, and that wine exerts its natural power upon kings. ... A poet overlooks the casual distinction of country and condition, as a painter, satisfied with the figure, neglects the drapery.[14]

Johnson here takes his stand on 'nature', that first principle which artists in the classical tradition sought to give expression to. In such a context, 'nature' is pre-eminently human nature conceived and ordered in a particular way; that is, dramatically, imaginatively, and yet, at the same time, objectively and impersonally. What Johnson's remarks suggest is Shakespeare's human centrality: his ability to provide a context for the actions of his characters; his ability to work, in an inward and non-reductive way, from different human centres. This is an achievement that might be described as classical, involving as it does, a peculiarly apt and dramatic tempering of human experience.

Joyce's description of the 'classical temper' in *Stephen Hero* is as follows:

The classical temper ... ever mindful of limitations, chooses rather to bend upon these present things and so to work upon them and fashion them that the quick intelligence may go beyond them to their meaning which is still unuttered. In this method the sane and joyful spirit issues forth and achieves imperishable perfection, nature assisting with her goodwill and thanks.[15]

Here we are aware both of a keen perception of form and of a peculiarly active kind of responsiveness.[16] And it is the vital interplay between these things which offers, I believe, the most fruitful approach to the topic of our Symposium. This is especially so when there exists a tension between the inherited form and creative innovation, or when the individual artist revitalizes and expands the possibilities of the tradition. It is in these terms that one can discuss the contribution of Andrea Gabrieli or Luca Marenzio to the Italian madrigal. Or again, the characteristic brilliance of Viennese classicism may be seen as the result of a successful integration of diverse material within an existing musical tradition.

The dictionary reminds us that the constitution, character or quality of a body was originally supposed to depend on the 'temper' or combination of its elements, and the derivation of the verb *temper* from Latin *temperare* seems to stress its appropriate conjunction with the 'classical': 'to divide or proportion duly, to mingle in due porportion, to combine properly . . . to arrange or keep in due measure or proportion' (*OED*). Seemingly a 'due measure or proportion' implies a special kind of ordering, some agreed coherence in the disposition or arrangement of parts.

During the period with which we are dealing, creative artists often aimed at a specially inclusive kind of ordering in their compositions, a fact evident from many of their titles: 'The Four Seasons' or 'The Seasons', 'The Creation', 'Paradise Lost', 'An Essay on Man'. In a word, they sought like Shakespeare's Puck to 'put a girdle round about the earth' by representing some aspect of history or human experience as of universal significance. Their sense of a rational ordering, of a physico-theology, could also, however, conceal darker possibilities, especially when sensuous experience threatened an independent life of its own, or when systems built by reason tended to prove vulnerable to it. Poussin's *Four Seasons* is a case in point. This series of paintings represents man's relationship to the elements and to time through a complex symbolism of myth and sacred history. Yet the fourth painting *Winter* of this series suggest a final cataclysm. The English poet James Thomson owes in his *Seasons* a recognizable debt to Poussin, even though his mode of expression may be regarded as other than classical; yet his reader is also conscious of the degree of strenuousness or effort with which Thomson seeks to express the different aspects of existence, and of man's place within these, as part of a larger and ordered whole.

Joseph Haydn was in turn indebted to a German translation of Thomson's poem in composing his last major work and second oratorio *The Seasons*, where the seasons are taken as a symbol or picture of human life. His first, enthusiastically acclaimed oratorio *The Creation* is reminiscent in its almost tangible optimism and virtuosity of the seventh book of Milton's *Paradise Lost*. This epic poem has avowedly a grand design, but one that neither precludes a sense of climax within the work, nor subordinates its richness of detail to the architectonic unity it is supposed to serve. For these and other reasons, not least the participation it seeks from the reader in its own enactment, the poem might appropriately be described as baroque. Perhaps its real interest may be said to lie in the fact that its subject escapes from the kind of control or purpose which its author, with at least one part of his mind, consciously sought to give it.

To move further back in time is to come upon a classical touchstone—Raphael's frescoes in the Vatican's Stanza della Segnatura ('the Room of the Signatures'). On the vault of this room are the figures of Law, Theology, Poetry and Philosophy, and the walls must be viewed in the light of the personifications enthroned on the ceiling, whose meanings radiate downwards. In the words of E. H. Gombrich, who has written illuminatingly of the whole, 'the Stanza will not stand fragmentation without complete disruption of its symbolic and artistic significance'.[17] Its controlled yet dynamic use of spatial harmonies aims at balancing a complete system of human life by bringing into an ideal relationship all aspects of man's existence. Raphael's work is replete with energy; at the same time, the overriding impression is one of equipoise, of individual forces held in a kind of equilibrium. Gombrich speaks not only of the detail of the composition in which 'every group, every gesture and every expression of the *Stanza* is indeed charged with significance'; he also speaks of the realization of the idea as 'infused' with Raphael's 'own kind of harmony and beauty, his own melodious groups and formal cadences':

> Once we grasp the general message we are led to find fresh metaphors and symbols in the rich configurations which surround us. We learn to see and to understand something of the numinous quality which Raphael and his contemporaries saw in Knowledge.[18]

The acknowledged classicism of this work resides, then, not merely in its manner or style, but in its energetic completeness of design and in what this therefore suggests. It may be said to point towards the furthest reach of the classical temper in its assumption that the person who is able to bring all its details into focus will have glimpsed the human ideal.

Notes

1. *Classical Influences on European Culture A.D. 1500–1700*, Cambridge, 1976, p. 27.
2. Cf. Bernard Smith, *The Antipodean Manifesto: Essays in Art and History*, Melbourne, 1976, pp. 126–7.
3. International Congress of the History of Art: *Studies in Western Art*, vol. iii: *Latin American Art, and the Baroque Period in Europe*, Princeton, New Jersey, 1963, p. 10.

4. *The Literary Works of Leonardo Da Vinci*, ed. J. P. Richter, London, 1970 (3rd edn), i. 56.

5. Daniel Mornet, *Histoire de la littérature et de la pensée françaises*, Paris, 1927, p. 75; quoted in Martin Turnell, *The Classical Moment*, London, 1947, p. 7.

6. *Stephen Hero*, ed. Theodore Spencer, London. 1956 (rev. edn), pp. 82, 83, 216.

7. *Xenophon: Recollections of Socrates and Socrates' Defense Before the Jury*, trans. Anna S. Benjamin, Indianapolis–New York, 1965, p. 93.

8. Quoted by Michael Greenhalgh, *The Classical Tradition in Art*, London, 1978, p. 89.

9. *Reflections on the Painting and Sculpture of the Greeks*, trans. Henry Fuseli, Scholar Press facsimile, Menston, 1972, pp. 12, 4.

10. *The Complete Works of Percy Bysshe Shelley*, ed. Roger Ingpen and Walter E. Peck, New York–London, 1965, vii. 115 ('A Defence of Poetry').

11. Quoted from Thomas Rymer's translation of the same year, *Reflections on Aristotle's Treatise of Poesie . . . by R. Rapin*, London, 1674, pp. 65–6.

12. *Institutio Oratoria*, XII, x, 14 ('*aridi et exsuci et exangues*').

13. *Complete Prose Works of John Milton*, gen. ed. D. M. Wolfe, New Haven–London, 1953– , ii. 405 (*Of Education*).

14. *Johnson on Shakespeare*, ed. Arthur Sherbo, New Haven–London, 1968 (vol. vii of the Yale Edition of the Works of Samuel Johnson), pp. 65–6.

15. *Stephen Hero*, p. 83.

16. S. L. Goldberg has described this as 'a responsive openness to life, a firm grasp on the centrally human, a respect for the present reality we all share . . .', *The Classical Temper: A Study of Joyce's Ulysses*, London, 1961, p. 32.

17. *Symbolic Images: Studies in the Art of the Renaissance*, New York–London, 1970, p. 88.

18. Ibid. p. 101.

1
Order, Grace and Terribilità:
The Achievement of
Italian High Renaissance Classicism

John Gregory

Despite recent controversy over its character and chronological limits, the art of the Italian High Renaissance remains a paradigm of classicism, as it was for many commentators from the seventeenth to the nineteenth centuries, culminating with Heinrich Wölfflin's study *Classic Art*, first published in 1899. In that book, written partly in revolt against much of the uncritical eulogy of earlier generations, Wölfflin determined to place discussion of the High Renaissance style on a firmer, almost 'scientific' footing, by means of precise analysis of its aesthetic and formal principles. Hence he devised a series of highly influential statements on the new 'ideals', 'beauty' and 'pictorial form', including pictorial principles such as 'simplification', 'mass', 'spaciousness', and 'unity and inevitability'.[1]

Even today, Wölfflin's analysis remains fundamental for most (if not all) students of the period (which for the purposes of this discussion I take to cover the years from about 1490 to 1540). But Wölfflin seems at times too close to his neoclassical forebears to allow the style of the High Renaissance full scope: he is fond of emphasizing the 'narrow limits' of the style, and in his introduction invites the reader to enter 'the high, still halls of classic art',[2] with just the trace of a Teutonic smile. For all its value, Wölfflin's exposition of High Renaissance principles ends up too much like a check-list of rules and regulations for greatness. More recent writing on the style has loosened the rigid framework of formal principles devised by Wölfflin, given stronger emphasis to the blending of ideal and naturalistic vision, and acknowledged the contribution of Venetian painting to the classic character of the period.[3]

Professor Hardy has remarked on one undoubted example of the classical, Raphael's *Stanza della Segnatura*, painted at the heart of the period, *c.* 1509–11. Formally speaking, the *School of Athens*

(Fig. 1) answers to almost all Wölfflin's principles: it is a work of masterly synthesis, the variety of individual figures and groups harmonized and controlled by the over-arching architecture, fullness of form matched at every point by spacious setting.[4] As Gombrich has emphasized too, form and content mesh perfectly in the work—the supreme harmony of the composition matches the idea of intellectual inquiry and achievement embodied so fulsomely and expressively in the figures of Plato and Aristotle, who control the philosophical character of the scene as they do its pictorial structure, from the vanishing point of the perspective construction. The classic comprehensiveness of the fresco, therefore, is as much a matter of thematic as formal control. Both form and content manifest a vision of order and expansive grandeur and an apparent ease in conjoining the most varied types and characters (drawn from several centuries of classical thought).[5]

In Venice, a parallel version of classicism emerged, predicated however on distinct if related formal and conceptual principles. One of the major revisions of the history of the High Renaissance in recent years has been the acknowledgement of the significance of Venetian painting to the classicism of the period, and research into the patterns of connection between the Venetian and Central Italian variants. Giorgione, for example, established in his Dresden *Venus* (1507-8) a sensuous equivalent to the harmonic perfection achieved by Raphael, but with forms mediated at every point by light and colour, in the context of a unity between human and natural existence never entirely matched in central Italy. Then Titian, in his first masterpiece the *Assunta* (completed in 1518), created a more dynamic harmonic mode, of rich and echoing tones which seem to match the glories of Venetian Cinquecento music. The composition is articulated as much by colour as by form, and in the figure of the Virgin one senses, as Bernard Berenson once wrote, a 'fullness of life' which marks this work too, for all its appeal to the Baroque, as another prime instance of classicism.[6]

One could continue with a recital of such paintings. But there are many works of the period which seem less obviously characteristic of 'classicism', at least in the terms in which it is often applied to the period. The Tempietto at S. Pietro in Montorio (Fig. 2)—designed by the major architect of the High Renaissance, Donato Bramante—is as perfect an example of ideal formal and conceptual unity as any classicism ever engendered. However, in the same years (around 1505) Bramante designed the so-called Belvedere (Fig. 3), linking the Vatican with Innocent VIII's villa some 300 metres to the north.[7] And this is quite a different affair, predicated not on ideals of harmonious centrality and balanced poise, but on principles closer to those Wölfflin and many others ascribe to the

Baroque: dynamic movement, fluidity, process and a taste for vast and expansive scale.[8] A preconception of the High Renaissance style as bounded by 'narrow limits' can scarcely accommodate such a work, and yet to exclude it from serious consideration is both historically and critically evasive. Faced with this type of evidence, the only real course is to draw a deep breath and ponder the issues anew. If this necessitates shedding some comforting generalizations, so be it; certainly that is preferable to re-shaping or ignoring certain facts to suit a prior definition of the period.

'Classicism', however it is defined for the period, must refer to much more than a relationship to antiquity. The High Renaissance is in some ways rather less close to the antique than certain artists before (for example, Mantegna) and after (for example, Giulio Romano, Raphael's pupil). Bramante's Belvedere, 'unclassical' in formal character, was based nevertheless on a precise attempt to resuscitate the nature of the villas of classical Rome.[9] The solution to this conundrum is perhaps to be found in Panofsky's eloquent suggestion that by contrast with their predecessors, High Renaissance artists 'succeeded in resurrecting the soul of antiquity instead of alternately galvanizing and exorcising its corpse'.[10] Michelangelo, for example, repeatedly demonstrates his capacity to penetrate to 'the soul of antiquity', and this is perhaps nowhere better evident than in his so-called 'Dying Slave' for the Tomb of Julius II, a work closely resembling in its marbled languor the Hellenistic Barberini Faun, excavated in Rome a century later.[11]

For this and other reaons, the theme of this seminar, 'the classical temper', seems particularly appropriate and helpful. It offers a path through the centuries of eulogy and analysis which still coat the High Renaissance, and need to be stripped away like old varnish. Above all, it seems to me essential to emphasize afresh the degree to which the period represents an adventurous flight of the spirit, a phase of inventiveness and varied achievement, not the mere apeing of antique precedent, or the exposition of narrow ideals and deadening formulae.

In subsequent centuries (in fact almost before the High Renaissance had ended) artists and theorists began to treat the period as a quarry for ideal forms and principles, but it is quite misleading to confuse these later critical perceptions with the ideas of the period itself. As Sidney Freedberg has remarked, '. . . it is this style's almost overriding principle that principle and actuality should fuse. Their interaction is a living one, by which idea is given substance in the particular event of art, while its substance is informed, conversely, by idea'; that is (to clarify Freedberg's language, once described as 'late Henry James retranslated from the German'), High Renaissance classicism works itself out as it goes.[12] Allowing for some exaggeration, this is a most important point. Like the classicism of fifth-century Greece, and unlike most later manifestations of classicism, the High Renaissance is avant-garde rather than conservative, and self-generating to a significant degree, despite the inspirational role played by aspects of antique art and theory in its development.

However, given the fact that the High Renaissance did not depend on a corpus of rule such as later classicism possessed, and notwithstanding the frequently noted absence of a consistent critical and theoretical language of art at the beginning of the sixteenth century, it is nonetheless true that this was a period during which the need for a developed 'theory of art' was becoming rapidly apparent, necessitated as it were by the sheer quantity and quality of art being created in Italy. During the Quattrocento, Alberti and Leonardo da Vinci addressed several fundamental theoretical issues, and at the same time (as recent studies by scholars such as Michael Baxandall have emphasized) the skeleton of a critical language was being assembled from sources as varied as classical rhetoric, commentaries on manners and the terminology of related arts such as dance. Then, during the first half of the Cinquecento, these varied threads were drawn together gradually by artists and commentators, finally being woven into firm patterns at mid-century by Vasari, Lodovico Dolce and others. From that point, in a sense, art theory never looked back.[13]

The scattered critical and theoretical views of the first part of the century, and the more resolved statements of Vasari in particular, furnish evidence of the major ideas circulating in the High Renaissance. Fidelity to nature, for example, is a central theme.[14] In the remainder of this paper I propose to consider the three major terms (or clusters of associated concepts), order, grace and *terribilità*, as a means of providing some sense of the ideals of the High Renaissance itself, and a clearer picture of the achievement of the artists of the period.

'Order' (Latin *ordo*) is so central a Renaissance concept that at times it is hardly emphasized—but of course it is a fundamental idea of which Leonardo da Vinci's 'Vitruvian Man' is almost a shorthand reminder. As used in the period, especially of art, it covers a wide range of things—from the simple arrangement of parts,[15] to a grand union of God, nature and man (particularly in Neoplatonic circles), and various shades in between.[16] In Leonardo da Vinci's art and thought, it takes the form of a comprehensive, 'organic' order unifying all things (except, perhaps, God), whereas for Michelangelo and his circle, it seemed to depend on the more intellectual idea of 'microcosm', whereby the single human figure could sum up all things.[17]

Although the concept of order is embedded in artistic theory and practice both before and after the High Renaissance, its potency as an ideal seems most apparent in the work of the High Renaissance masters. Bramante's Tempietto, as already remarked, summarizes order in the purest form. So too, on a far grander scale, did Bramante's initial scheme for the rebuilding of St. Peter's. The surviving half-plan and the foundation medal of 1506 reveal a structure founded on the circle, rising through ordered stages to the massive dome above. This is order akin to the idea of organic form which obsessed Leonardo, and Bramante's scheme closely recalls a number of sketches of centralized churches made by Leonardo in the years when both he and Bramante lived in Milan.[18] Leonardo's forms cluster and cohere, whereas Bramante's are grandly, almost starkly, monumental; but the connections are clear.

It is but a short step from the clustering half-domes of Leonardo's architectural sketches to compositions of his later Florentine period, such as the Burlington Cartoon, where figures and limbs interweave in sometimes startling fashion. The connecting link is nature, the source of order for Leonardo. During his later career in particular, phenomena seem to intersect and overlap in his eyes, so that human hair, plants and the movements of water all conform to the same barely comprehensible patterns. Eventually, or so Kenneth Clark has argued, the effort becomes too much: nature's order seems to defeat even Leonardo's genius—at least one may read in this way the late drawings in which the natural order is overturned in a deluge of shattering power, depicted with astonishing linear complexity.[19]

Almost twenty years earlier, however, Leonardo painted what remains a paradigm of the classic style at its most ordered, his *Last Supper*. Here the controlling principles are Christ's eucharistic role, and the idea of an emotional and expressive ordering of experience, as the disciples react to the news that one of them will betray him.[20] In their varying reactions (once much clearer, as the preparatory drawings reveal), the apostles cohere into loosely balanced groups which suggest in a most subtle way the weighty issues momentarily in the balance here. To register only the 'unity and inevitability' of the formal composition, as Wölfflin did, is to undercut the greatness of the work, and in fact to ignore its powerful classicism—in that the balance and harmony summed up in Christ (placed at the vanishing point of the perspective construction, the device later adapted by Raphael in the *School of Athens*) are counterpoised by the potential for collapse of this ordered vision.[21]

The collapse of order specifically envisaged in Leonardo's late drawings is not necessarily 'unclassical'. Vasari quotes Michelangelo as saying, in characteristically dry fashion, 'If life pleases us, death ought not to displease us, being from the hand of the same master.'[22] The critical distinction is that Michelangelo's vision encompassed God as the ultimate source of order, whereas Leonardo's atheism allowed him no such solace. Nevertheless, Michelangelo's sometimes despairing response to existence, as evident from his letters and poetry, suggests that his conception of the nature of things was no less complex than Leonardo's. David Summers, in a massive and absorbing recent study of Michelangelo, has argued in fact that his art and thought oscillated throughout his career between the two irreconcilable poles of 'fantasy' and 'order'. The classic resolution could only be made intellectually, in theory, as it was by one of Michelangelo's circle Vincenzo Danti: 'If there were no disorder the order would not be known, inasmuch as natural disorder is a means of making known the divine order and human disorder of making known the natural order.'[23]

Under the umbrella of Christian certainties, order seems a natural habit of mind for the early Michelangelo, and, in vastly different form, for him in his old age. But in the middle period of his life (the years, incidentally, when his poetic activity and interest in theoretical issues seem strongest) tensions are most apparent. In the Medici Chapel, for example (essentially a work of the 1520s), sculpture and architecture, though both Michelangelo's own, seem ill at ease in the lower sections of the work: only in the upper area of the dome is there some sense of resolution in the perfected architectual forms.[24] In the roughly contemporary Laurentian library, Michelangelo exploited the expressive contrast between the tense and in certain respects undeniably anti-classical architecture of the vestibule (for example the columns, apparently embedded in the wall and carrying no load), and the serene repose of the reading room. Sometimes read as a prime instance of 'Mannerism', the net result of the whole seems to be much more a species of classicism, whereby order is emphasized by means of a process, in which the lack of order and repose in the entrance room prepares the visitor for the demonstration of classical values beyond.[25]

In this discussion of 'order', the most obvious exemplar, Raphael, has not been mentioned, but his adherence to the principle hardly needs detailed discussion. And if his belief in order is obvious, his espousal of the ideal of 'grace' (*grazia*) is even more manifest.

'Grace' is a critical term with a long and interesting history, and it became one of the most significant terms with which sixteenth-century theorists such as Vasari characterized the artistic achievement of their own time. In the earlier part of the century, its most influential exposition was given not by an artist or art-theorist, but by Baldassare Castiglione, in the context of his book on manners, *The Courtier*. There Castiglione spoke of the supreme virtue of grace, a gift of nature, beyond learning, but attainable to some degree by the practice of careless ease (*sprezzatura*), avoiding everything forced and affected, and using art to conceal art.[26]

It is hardly accidental that Castiglione was portrayed by Raphael, with whom he was well-acquainted, for Raphael above all his contemporaries in the arts exemplified this easiness and grace of which Castiglione wrote shortly afterwards. In later centuries, these qualities of Raphael's art became something of a millstone to his reputation; by the nineteenth century both his life and art were coated by a thick sugary veneer which gave rise to a number of unutterably sickly verbal and visual fantasies.[27] To some extent, Raphael's reputation even now remains tarnished by the excesses of his later admirers.

In the Cinquecento, however, his qualities were admired and emulated with a good deal more understanding. And it was Raphael's possession of *grazia* above all which was so admired. Vasari had no hesitation in calling Raphael 'the most graceful' of all his contemporaries.[28] Then in 1557, Ludovico Dolce published his *Aretino*, which included a highly influential paragone between Michelangelo and Raphael, the latter being declared the greater by virtue of his grace and ease.[29]

'Grace' here, it must be stressed, means a number of things, but least of all the sort of thing we might take it to mean from modern usage. It was not simply that Raphael's style often displayed extraordinary sweetness and lightness of touch (although this is commonly the case with his female figures in particular), but that in whatever he painted, the most complex solutions appeared somehow natural, inevitable, and yet unforced. A classic example is the *Madonna della Sedia* (Fig. 4), a work of Raphael's full Roman maturity. The fulsome monumentality of forms might not match our modern idea of grace, but the ease with which this congregation of limbs is accommodated to the circular (*tondo*) setting exemplifies Cinquecento *grazia* in a most refined way. Raphael's characteristic search for pure rhythmic cadences in the variety of nature, evident in the numerous Madonna compositions of his earlier career, attains here a clarity and classic ease which explains the picture's fame. And a better demonstration could scarcely be found of Castiglione's dictum that perfect grace consists in the use of art to conceal art.[30]

Dolce's view that Raphael's achievement transcended Michelangelo's might be emphasized by comparing Michelangelo's own essays in the *tondo* form during the first decade of the sixteenth century. Certainly the *Doni Tondo* (Fig. 5) of about 1503–4 presents a marked contrast to Raphael's work: Michelangelo's figures engage in a most energetic display of activity (compare the tensed, aggressive arm of the Virgin extending across the centre of the group, with the same motif, easy and relaxed, in Raphael), and the style itself is aggressive and hard-edged, the colours harshly metallic, by contrast with the softened tones and muted edges in the Raphael. In the 1520s, Paolo Giovio made the same sort of comparison, concluding that in this capacity for 'mixing and mitigating the starkness of the more vivid pigments', Raphael indeed surpassed Michelangelo.[31] In these terms, too, Vasari's description of Leonardo da Vinci as possessed of *grazia divina*[32] is perfectly comprehensible. Not only did Leonardo's art, like his own personality and manners, reveal grace (thus Vasari remarks of Leonardo that his 'every movement was grace itself'),[33] but the softened *sfumato* for which he was renowned manifested that grace in the very pictorial surface of his works.

Grazia, however, is also listed by Vasari as one of Michelangelo's prime qualities, and here plainly it means something rather different. Vasari uses it in particular of the composition of the human figure, which Michelangelo achieved '. . . with the most complete grace and absolute perfection'.[34] Thus a figure like the Sistine *Adam*, so characteristically chiselled in its outline, nonetheless displays *grazia*, and many other figures on the Sistine Ceiling exemplify the quality even more clearly. In the marvellous *Libyan Sibyl*, Michelangelo seems to come close to Raphael's own capacity for composing a figure of extraordinary complexity in an easy and ideally harmonious fashion. The surviving sheet of preparatory sketches in red chalk reveals the 'art' (again in Castiglione's sense) underlying this masterpiece.[35]

Pope, in his *Essay on Criticism* (1711), gave voice to the sense 'grace' had attained during the seventeenth century, in the eloquent phrase, 'a grace beyond the reach of art'. As Samuel Monk has observed, in an exemplary study of the term, 'grace' had become for later classicism a type of escape clause from the restrictions of rules, a *je ne sais quoi* which was the final, indefinable proof of greatness; thus, in the same passage, Pope speaks of the 'nameless graces which no methods teach'.[36] In the early sixteenth century, with critical language still very much in a process of gestation and 'the rules' looming in the unseen future, there was little need for such an escape clause, but *grazia* does already carry this connotation. Thus Vasari, in a phrase prefiguring Pope's, speaks of 'grace beyond measure' as one of the crucial qualities of the modern style; as Anthony Blunt observes, *grazia* for Vasari is 'an indefinable quality dependent on judgement and therefore on the eye'.[37] For us, as for Vasari, this remains a fundamental High Renaissance achievement, corresponding to the self-confident creativity of the style; but it might be pointed out in passing that it became a two-edged sword as the century progressed. Even in the later works of Raphael, *grazia* and its concomitants, 'ease', 'facility', 'licence' and 'fantasy', carry the threat of becoming less truly liberating qualities. By the time Vasari made his notorious claim that a proof of the perfection of art at mid-century was the fact 'that where the first masters took six years to paint one picture, our masters today would only take one year to paint six',[38] the drawbacks are becoming clear. But that belongs to a different, if not unrelated issue.

Terribilità, like 'order' and 'grace', arises from the terminology of ancient rhetorical theory, and carries a range of related meanings. But of the three terms, it is most obviously associated with the High Renaissance, and in particular with one man, Michelangelo.[39] We tend to use it rather loosely, but understandably, to define the awesome power of such figures as the *Moses*, who could be described, in the framework of this seminar, as in a terrible classical temper!

The explosive and provocative nature of Michelangelo's personality is well known, though his later biographers Condivi and Vasari tended to play down the more extreme aspects of his character. Paolo Giovio, in the 1520s, was less inhibited, and wrote in his short life of Michelangelo:

> . . . while a man of so great genius, he was by nature so rough and untamed that, beyond the incredible scandals of his private life, he even begrudged posterity successors in his art; for even when implored by princes he could never be induced to instruct, or even to admit anyone at all to his workshop for the sake of observing.[40]

The term *terribilità* is first used of Michelangelo in this context in a letter by Sebastiano del Piombo of about 1520. Leo X, whose court revolved essentially around the ideal of *grazia*, had remarked: 'He is terrible, Michelangelo; as you see, one can do nothing with him'; to which Sebastiano replied that Michelangelo's *terribilità* was a result of the greatness of his art.[41] Hence *terribilità*, applied first to Michelangelo perhaps in its negative sense of 'dreadful', is transformed into a far more positive and laudatory aesthetic term. It carries other connotations too, not merely of intensity and force, but also of abundant skill, heroic style, and boundless artistic capacity.[42]

Vasari uses the terms *terribile* and *terribilità* of a number of artists, from Donatello to Tintoretto (which reveals its range of meanings), and also of works of art, and of patrons. In his own lifetime, Pope Julius II was referred to as a *natura terribile*, and in a revealing passage in the life of Bramante, Vasari remarks that Julius II chose Bramante, blest with a 'terrible genius', to undertake the 'most grand and terrible building of St. Peter's'.[43] But it was above all Michelangelo of whom the term was used. It encompassed that 'forceful air' of his figures against which Dolce's *Aretino* placed Raphael's grace by preference;[44] but it also expressed the sense of amazing skill at Michelangelo's disposal. Thus, in a curious way, the extremes of *grazia* and *terribilità* meet, for underlying both was the idea of extraordinary skill in handling the most difficult artistic feats.[45]

In the Sistine Ceiling, all these varied shades of meaning of *terribilità* meet and cohere. Commissioned by the 'terrible' Julius II, and at certain points powerfully evocative of that Pope's warlike zeal,[46] this work matched the tremendousness of theme, the beginnings of the world and the promise of Christ's salvation, with an encompassing *terribilità*, a stylistic and compositional completeness which astonished Michelangelo's contemporaries. Vasari, for example, remarked of the *Creation of Sun and Moon* that the power of its subject was matched by the great skill of fore-shortening;[47] and of the climactic figure of the prophet *Jonah* (Fig. 6) he wrote:

> But who can see without wonder and amazement the tremendousness (*terribilità*) of Jonah, the last figure of the chapel, for the vaulting which curves forward from the wall is made by a triumph of art to appear straight, through the posture of the figure, which by the mastery of the drawing and the light and shade, appears really to be bending backwards.[48]

The emphasis on skill in these passages may not strike as strong a chord with us now, but the ideal comprehensiveness encompassed by the term *terribilità* does come close to the continued response the Ceiling evokes. Paolo Giovio called it simply 'a testimony of absolute art',[49] and it remains for many *the* work of art, casting a kind of mesmeric spell over the hordes who shuffle reverently through the Sistine Chapel, pausing occcasionally to defy the guards by shooting off a hopelessly optimistic flash photo with their Insta-matics. I would suggest that they are responding, if sometimes unwittingly, to the majesty of the greatest achievement of the High Renaissance, a blend of order, grace and *terribilità* which reveals potently the real scope and achievement of this period of classic art.

Notes

1. *Classic Art*, London, 1952, trans. P. and L. Murray. Herbert Read's Introduction to this edition includes discussion of the 'scientific' approach of Wölfflin.

2. Ibid. pp. 244 and xv.

3. M. Levey, *High Renaissance*, Harmondsworth, 1975, criticizes Wölfflin freely, and emphasizes the Venetian contribution. More recently, C. H. Smyth has specified aspects of the role of Venice, whilst retaining the broad terms of Wölfflin's account; see 'Venice and the Emergence of the High Renaissance in Florence: Observations and Questions', in *Florence and Venice: Comparisions and Relations*, Florence, 1979, i. 208–49, esp. p. 217. The theme of a blend of idealism and naturalism dominates the account of S. Freedberg, *Painting of the High Renaissance in Rome and Florence*, Harvard, 1961.

4. Wölfflin, pp. 93–6.

5. E. H. Gombrich, *Symbolic Images: Studies in the Art of the Renaissance*, New York–London, 1970, pp. 85 ff.

6. *The Italian Painters of the Renaissance*, London, 1952, p. 19. For the recent emphasis on Venice, see Levey and Smyth as cited above (n. 3), and S. Freedberg, *Painting in Italy, 1500–1600*, Pelican History of Art, Harmondsworth, 1971, chs. 2, 5.

7. The dating is somewhat uncertain. I follow A. Bruschi, *Bramante*, London, 1977, p. 196, suggesting 1504–5 ff. for the Belvedere (following Ackerman), and *c*. 1505–6 ff. for the Tempietto proper (the inscription date, 1502, perhaps refers to the crypt below).

8. Bruschi, passim (but esp. pp. 177 ff.). Wöfflin's most influential statements on the supposed contrasts between Renaissance and Baroque styles appear in his *Principles of Art History*, New York, 1950 (first published in 1915).

9. Bruschi, pp. 87 ff., and J. Ackerman, 'The Belvedere as a Classical Villa', *Journal of the Warburg and Courtauld Institutes*, xiv (1951), 70–91.

10. E. Panofsky, *Renaissance and Renascences in Western Art*, Copenhagen, 1960, p. 205.

11. For the Barberini Faun (Munich, Glyptothek), discovered in Rome between 1624 and 1628, see F. Haskell and N. Penny, *Taste and the Antique: the Lure of Classical Sculpture 1500–1900*, New Haven–London, 1981, pp. 202–5 (Cat. no. 33). Professor Peter Tomory informs me that small versions of a similar type were circulating in the sixteenth century.

12. S. Freedberg, *Painting in Italy*, p. 4; the description of Freedberg's style is attributed to Freedberg himself in the review by H. Zerner, 'Mind your Maniera', *New York Review of Books*, 31 August 1972, p. 25.

13. A. Blunt, *Artistic Theory in Italy, 1450–1600*, Oxford, 1940; see M. Baxandall, *Giotto and the Orators: Humanist Observers of Painting in Italy and the Discovery of Pictorial Composition 1350–1450*, Oxford, 1971; and M. Baxandall, *Painting and Experience in Fifteenth Century Italy*, Oxford, 1972.

14. Levey, p. 18, acknowledges the importance of this concept for Vasari (notwithstanding Levey's central contention that the High Renaissance is concerned fundamentally with art outdoing nature). For a recent restatement of the continuing significance of *mimesis* in the sixteenth century (*contra* Shearman and others), see H. Miedema, 'On Mannerism and *maniera*', *Simiolus*, x (1979), 19–45, esp. 22 ff. A typical example from earlier in the century is Paolo Giovio's praise of Michelangelo's Sistine Ceiling, written in the 1520s; see T. Price Zimmermann, 'Paolo Giovio and the Evolution of Renaissance Art Criticism', in *Cultural Aspects of the Italian Renaissance: Essays in honour of Paul Oskar Kristeller*, ed. C. Clough, New York, 1976, p. 416 and n. 50.

15. For a representative example, see Baxandall, *Giotto and the Orators*, pp. 48, 62.

16. D. Summers, *Michelangelo and the Language of Art*, Princeton, 1981, p. 299, quotes Ficino and discusses the concept further. P. Barocchi (ed.), *Scritti d'arte del Cinquecento*, Milan–Naples, 1973, ii, 1715 ff. (sect. XI, 'Proporzione, Misura, Giudizio'), prints several relevant passages, including an extract from Vincenzo Danti.

17. Cf. Summers, pp. 285 ff.

18. For example, Paris Institut de France, Ms F. fol. 17ᵛ; see A. Popham, *The Drawings of Leonardo da Vinci*, London, 1946, no. 312. For the relations between Bramante and Leonardo generally, see L. Heydenreich, 'Leonardo and Bramante', in *Leonardo's Legacy*, ed. C. O'Malley, Berkeley, 1969, pp. 124 ff.

19. K. Clark, *Leonardo da Vinci*, Harmondsworth, 1967 (rev. edn), esp. pp. 14–16.

20. Or, as one of my students once wrote, *portray* him—which gives a nice twist to the disciples' shocked reaction!

21. Wölfflin, *Classic Art*, pp. 23 ff., 279 ff. L. Steinberg, 'Leonardo's *Last Supper*', *Art Quarterly*, xxxvii (1973), 297–410, gives the fullest statement of the actual and perceived complexities of the composition and iconography.

22. Quoted by Summers, p. 209.

23. Quoted and discussed by Summers, p. 309. See also pp. 447 ff. A distinction needs to be made between the Christian idea of 'order' in the Renaissance, and the 'natural order' envisaged by the Enlightenment; see M. Foucault, *The Order of Things*, New York, 1973, pp. 50–8.

24. Recent research has emphasized Michelangelo's central role in planning both architecture and sculpture from the start of the project; see C. Elam, 'The Site and Early Building History of Michelangelo's New Sacristy', *Mitteilungen des Kunsthistorischen Instituts in Florenz*, xxiii (1979), 155–86; also Summers, p. 544, n. 34.

25. J. Ackerman, *The Architecture of Michelangelo*, Harmondsworth, 1970, p. 121; Ackerman also emphasizes a 'dynamic' quality to

Michelangelo's architecture generally (e.g. p. 279). Cf. J. Shearman, *Mannerism*, Harmondsworth, 1967, pp. 74–5.

26. For discussion of Castiglione's remarks, see S. Monk, 'A Grace beyond the reach of Art', *Journal of the History of Ideas*, v (1944), 131–50 (esp. 139–40); also P. Barocchi, ii. 1611 ff. (sect. X: 'Bellezza e Grazia').

27. See J. Pope-Hennessy, *Raphael*, New York–London, 1970, pp. 9–37 (e.g. fig. 6: engraving by E. Eichens of 'The Child Raphael').

28. *Le Opere di Giorgio Vasari*, ed. G. Milanesi, Florence, 1906, iv. 11 ('... piu di tutti il graziosissimo Raffaello da Urbino').

29. M. Roskill, *Dolce's 'Aretino' and Venetian Art Theory of the Cinquecento*, New York, 1968, pp. 174–7 (text and translation of Dolce's treatise).

30. See E. H. Gombrich, 'Raphael's Madonna della Sedia', in *Norm and Form*, London, 1966, pp. 64–80; M. Levey, pp. 45–8.

31. Price Zimmermann, p. 417.

32. *Le Opere*, ed. Milanesi, iv. 11.

33. Ibid. iv. 17; the translation is that of A. Hinds (see G. Vasari, *The Lives of the Painters, Sculptors and Architects*, London, 1963, ii. 156).

34. *Le Opere*, iv. 17 (trans. Hinds, ed. cit. ii. 155).

35. Metropolitan Museum of Art, New York. See C. de Tolnay, *Corpus dei disegni di Michelangelo*, Novara, 1975–80, i. 156ʳ.

36. See Monk, passim, esp. pp. 131, 146, 150.

37. *Le Opere*, iv. 9 (trans. Hinds, ii. 152); Blunt, p. 93.

38. *Le Opere*, iv. 13 (with a dry editorial aside; trans. Hinds, ii. 154).

39. Summers, pp. 234–41; see also J. Bialostocki, *'Terribilità', Stil und Überlieferung in der Kunst des Abendlandes. Akten des 21. Int. Kongr. f. Kunstgeschichte*, Berlin, 1967, iii. 222–5, who traces the connection of the term with related concepts in Greek and Roman rhetoric.

40. Price Zimmermann, p. 416.

41. Quoted and discussed, together with a second letter by Sebastiano, in Summers, p. 235.

42. See n. 39.

43. *Le Opere*, iv. 160–61; cf. Summers, p. 240.

44. See n. 29.

45. For the relation of *terribilità* to *difficultà*, see Summers, p. 234.

46. F. Hartt, *'Lignum vitae in medio paradisi*: the Stanze d'Eliodoro and the Sistine Ceiling', *Art Bulletin*, xxxii (1950), 215–18, relates the character and physiognomy of Julius II to the image of the creating deity in the later narrative section of the Ceiling.

47. G. Vasari, *La vita di Michelangelo nelle redazioni del 1550 e del 1568*, ed. P. Barocchi, Milan–Naples, 1962, i. 43.

48. Ibid. i. 51 (trans. Hinds, ed. cit. iv. 130); see also Summers, pp. 240–1.

49. Price Zimmermann, p. 415 and n. 53 (*absolutae artis testimonium*).

2
'Est modus in rebus'
The Decline and Fall of
the Classical Italian Madrigal

John Steele

The classical moment in the history of any style of art is apt to be brief. It seldom persists beyond about three or four decades before changing ideas and tastes introduce disturbances that will tilt against the ideal of classical balance, emphasizing certain elements of the art work at the expense of others, stressing passionate sensation above coherence of form, virtuosity of technique above grace and elegance of expression. To the artists of the new generation the classical ideal will often seem cold and artificial, though still perhaps worthy of a respect not untinged with a degree of irony. Yet most of those who resist the new anti-classical styles, seeking to perpetuate the classical ideal, will as often as not be reduced to mere classicizing in their attempts to continue with forms whence the substance has all but fled. Only a very few individual artists of the highest stature who succeed a classical period will be able to forge a personal style that, while admitting some features of the new, will remain essentially classical, self-contained and characteristically inimitable. One thinks of such artists as Michelangelo, Titian, William Byrd, Sebastian Bach, and Beethoven. All produced their later work in what one might plausibly describe as a 'post-classical' period, all created works of art which are amongst the highest achievements of our civilization, and none had much appreciable direct influence on the work of later generations. Their styles not only were too individual to be imitated beyond the stage of mere plagiarism or parody, but also must have seemed at once old-fashioned and difficult to their younger contemporaries.

The great classical achievement of sixteenth-century. Italian music was the madrigal. Its ramifications for the extension of western musical sensibility were vast. Its composers' discoveries and experiments revealed that music could be an expressive as well as a semiological art, and the future development of western music would have been unimaginable without their example. Yet in the process of the madrigal's seventy-year reign, attitudes changed, and opposed ideals as to the nature of musical expression destroyed the madrigal itself as a paradigm of the unity between poetry and music. It is the purpose of this paper to examine the nature of the classical madrigal and to explain the reasons for its decline and fall.

Let me begin with the first part of my title, completing the quotation whence it is drawn: 'There is a measure in all things. There are, in short, fixed bounds, beyond and short of which right can find no place.'[1] This was quoted by the Bolognese musical theorist Giovanni Maria Artusi in his famous attack on certain licences in the madrigals of Claudio Monteverdi.[2] Artusi wrote from the point of view of a well-versed but not blindly dogmatic classicist.[3] He was a devoted follower of the greatest musical theorist of the late Renaissance, Gioseffe Zarlino, and had made in his *Seconda parte dell'arte del contrapunto*, printed in Venice in 1589, a distinguished and original contribution towards dissonance theory, based on a close study of the practice of his contemporaries.[4] What he feared in Monteverdi's novel, unprepared and unresolved dissonances was a threat to the whole tissue of classical polyphony. In this he was correct, and the date of the publication of his attack is ironically the very year—1600—that most modern music historians arbitrarily set for the dawn of the Baroque era.

Licentious dissonance, however, was not the only threat to the traditional polyphonic style. By the end of the century, two others had already come to fruition: the cults of the virtuoso and of monody.

To understand this triple threat, we must first look at the classical madrigal itself, and understand something of its range within the limits of the central language of sixteenth-century musical style. To do this properly would require far more space than I have available here; Alfred Einstein needed three volumes and even then omitted much. I am conscious also that in a paper of this kind I cannot afford to become abstrusely technical, lest I lose your good will as I would surely become enmeshed in a pedantic web of detail. So perhaps I may be pardoned if I approach the subject from an angle of aesthetic attitudes and trends, and bring in technical matters only in so far as they illuminate the artistic aims of the madrigal composers themselves.

First I must briefly sketch the history of the madrigal. The exact origin and meaning of the word as it appeared in fourteenth-century Italy is unknown; it is in any case immaterial to our study of the sixteenth-century madrigal. For our purposes, the madrigal is simply a part-song, a through-composed setting of various poetic forms for a balanced group of from three to eight solo voices. The poetry chosen is often of high literary merit, and since the classical madrigal is intimately involved with literary values, some discussion of these is inevitable here.

In 1501, the Venetian humanist, poet, and later cardinal Pietro Bembo produced an edition of the *Canzoniere* of the fourteenth-century Tuscan poet Petrarch. The following year he published an edition of Dante. As James Haar writes: 'Both are volumes of fundamental importance in Italian philology and represent the foundation of Bembo's interest in Tuscan as a literary language.'[5] Bembo's influence, and his model of Petrarch as the ideal of Italian lyric poetry, were decisive. Dante, although occasionally set by the madrigalists, was thought too harsh and rigid compared with the delicate effects and variation of rhyme, rhythm and imagery found in Petrarch. Petrarch's subject-matter too was more attractive to the composer in search of settable texts, in particular the sentimental, spiritualized effusions to the living but unattainable Laura, or the anguished laments after her death. The madrigalists return time and again to Petrarch. It was his inspiration that sparked the form, and some of the last of the great madrigal books, such as Marenzio's ninth book of 1599, contain superb settings of his verse. Of the host of more modern poets favoured by the madrigalists, I have space here to mention only two: Sannazaro and Ariosto. Jacopo Sannazaro, a Neapolitan humanist, started the Renaissance pastoral fashion with his *Arcadia*, a novel with verse eclogues after the manner of Virgil, written in 1481, but not published until 1502. He found many imitators, the most important of whom came much later in the century. Sannazaro remained nevertheless Marenzio's favourite poet. Ludovico Ariosto was popular with musicians throughout the century and well beyond; stanzas and themes of his epic *Orlando Furioso* (1516), at once comic and heroic, were a treasure-house for composers of madrigals and then of opera for generations to come. He was, as Alfred Einstein said, the only very great Italian poet of the century.[6]

The early madrigalists developed their musical techniques of verse setting out of the Italian frottola style, with a judicious admixture of northern, Franco-Flemish, polyphony and the Parisian chanson.[7] The frottola had been essentially a light refrain and strophic form, not through-composed, though latterly it admitted settings of Petrarchan sonnets and canzona stanzas. Most frottole are, although written in four parts, essentially solo songs with a supporting instrumental bass part and inner parts written in a kind of pseudo-polyphony. In the case of performance accompanied by lute alone, one of these inner parts could even be dispensed with altogether.[8] What we have in fact is a kind of prototype monody which disappears from sight, swamped by the madrigal for about seventy years. It emerges again, transformed and triumphant, at the end of the century, and was perhaps after all the true mainstream of native Italian music which continued unabated from the seventeenth to the twentieth century, the madrigal itself being nothing but a beautiful aberration.

For it is true that nearly all the early madrigal composers were northerners, *oltremontani* from France and the Netherlands, and northerners such as Willaert, Rore, Lasso, Monte and Wert dominate the progression of the madrigal almost until its very end.[9] Only as latecomers do Italians such as Andrea Gabrieli and Luca Marenzio introduce a new note of voluptuous hedonism into the classical madrigal.

The man who did more than any other to establish the dominance of the northern polyphonic style over the developing madrigal was Adrian Willaert. A pupil of Mouton in Paris, he arrived in Rome by 1515, and was in the service of the Este family, the rulers of Ferrara, from 1515 until 1527. In 1527 Willaert was appointed *maestro di cappella* at St Mark's in Venice and remained there until his death in 1562. From this vantage, through his unsurpassed contrapuntal technique, the quantity and scope of his music, his concern for matching word and tone, and his myriad pupils, he wielded a decisive influence on the received musical style—the *stile osservato* —of the late Renaissance. This is the style analyzed and codified by his pupil Zarlino in the *Istitutioni harmoniche* of 1558, the standard work on late Renaissance music theory and practice.

Willaert took over the early madrigal as it had been established by Verdelot and others in the 1520s and early 1530s and transformed it. In the hands of its originators the madrigal had been essentially a development of the fully-texted frottola style (that is, with words underlaid to all four vocal parts), only lightly contrapuntal, the melodic interest concentrated in the top part and the music closely following the line divisions and rhythms of the verse. We still sometimes find the same music being used for new words within the same piece. Attempts at word-painting in music were still minimal, clear declamation being more highly valued. Willaert's aim was to apply the weightier, asymmetrical flow of northern counterpoint, to interpret the Italian verse stanza almost in terms of the motet. He scrupulously tailored each voice part to the sense and declamation of the words, in the process ignoring the line-endings and rhythm of the verse. Homophony is still used to point up crucial words and phrases, but the essential background of the style is imitative counterpoint, carefully worked through all the voices.

Although Willaert was also interested in the lighter forms such as the villanesca (which lie beyond the scope of this paper), his serious madrigals, including some of the earliest cycles of Petrarch, are perhaps too serious, the expression too undifferentiated, to arouse much more than historical interest today. His immediate successors, however, could not afford to ignore his severe example, the subsequent history of the madrigal consisting in a large part in how they came to terms with it.

With Willaert's star pupil Cipriano de Rore the classical moment of the madrigal is reached. Another Fleming, he was in Italy perhaps by the age of twenty, in 1536. Six years later his first book of madrigals for five voices appeared; from this time on, five voices was the norm for the classical madrigal. More modern-looking notation is also adopted. *Note nere* or *misura cromatica* has nothing to do with chromaticism in our sense, but means that the unit of beat has shifted from the minim to the crotchet, a style of notation occasionally found also in the Parisian chanson, one which encourages a lighter, faster movement and one which is more easily understood by amateur performers. The old, white-note style remains alongside the new, however, but now tends to be reserved for madrigals of serious and poignant expression, especially by later composers such as Marenzio.

In his maturing years as a madrigalist Rore worked mainly in Ferrara, a city which, together with nearby Mantua, was the most progressive centre for secular music in Italy for virtually the entire late Renaissance. We can observe how Rore gradually refines his style, admitting in each succeeding book a more rigorous declamation of the text with a marvellously supple homophony that never yet totally rejects the resources of counterpoint or good part-writing. He was well aware of the chromatic experiments of his friend Vicentino—they had been fellow pupils of Willaert—but Rore's excursions into chromaticism never sound experimental and contrived, but simply a logical extension of his impressive powers of musical imagery. Nor did his fundamentally serious nature despise gaiety: his lightness of touch with the naughty verse by Alfonso d'Avalos, *Anchor che col partire*, ensured its success as perhaps the most popular madrigal ever written. It was admired, imitated, transcribed for instruments, and was even used for a parody mass by Philippe de Monte and a Magnificat by Lasso. It was Rore too who was mainly responsible for forging much of the conventional musical language of the madrigal that was later to be so bitterly attacked by Vincenzo Galilei. He did not even disdain occasionally to employ 'eye-music' to afford the singers some harmless amusement. Renaissance 'imitation of nature' is now extended to the notation itself, and later composers will represent night and darkness with black notes, eyes with a pair of level semibreves. They will also indulge in elaborate solmization puns so that verbal phrases such as 'mi fa lasso' may be represented in the music by the appropriate notes of the hexachord:

mi   fa   las-so

The madrigalists have been blamed for triviality, since much of this sort of thing is inaudible to listeners and is in any case mere symbolism and has nothing to do with affective expression. But this is just the point; the classical madrigal is directed not primarily to listeners, but to cultivated amateur performers.

Let us consider one of Rore's finest madrigals. *Da le belle contrade d'Oriente* appeared in his last book for five voices, published in 1566, the year after he died. The publisher Gardano wrote in his dedication to the Duke of Parma (where Rore had held his last appointment) that Rore united the traditions of 'Josquin, the delightful invention of modulation and fine singing, Mouton, the true art of variation of counterpoint, and Adrian Willaert, the continuity of sweet harmony'.[10] We do not know who wrote the text of this extraordinarily sensual sonnet. A detailed analysis of Rore's word-setting would be out of the question here, but I must point out just a few of its subtleties.

Rore has achieved a setting which is the height of the classical madrigal technique in its balance between the conflicting demands of the text and of musical design. The conventional imitative opening is followed by a vivid evocation of Venus arising from the sea. After the frankly declamatory treatment of the phrase 'Fruiva in braccio al divin idol mio', there is a purely musical reminiscence of Venus arising at the words 'che non caper humana mente'. This alternation of elaborate polyphony and homophonic declamation persists throughout the work in a clear musical design. Rore begins too by painting the images of whole verbal phrases in music, only later focusing on individual key words. Venus accuses: 'you go', questioningly to an upward interval; 'alas', to a downward interval; 'you leave me alone', to a more anguished, chromatic movement upwards; and 'farewell' confirms the drooping, downward interval of 'alas'. Then there are the astonishing sharpward 'modulations' for the agony of 'what will become of me?', soon balanced by the equally remarkable flatward ones for 'how uncertain and brief your sweetness'. After these distant excursions, the last twenty-five bars of the music contain no accidentals at all, but reconfirm the original key of F. But 'she clung to me tight' is set in close imitative *stretto*, and the knots and the acanthus are related in deft musical melismas.

After Rore, the madrigal still had about forty years to run. There were several lines of development, complex to describe, since these are often found in the work of one composer (Orlando di Lasso and Philippe de Monte, fellow Flemings with Rore, are cases in point). Rather than describing these, I shall instead deal briefly with Andrea Gabrieli, who set the tone for the light-hearted, pastoral style of madrigal for the rest of the century. Andrea was another pupil of Willaert, but he has little in common with his master. An accomplished contrapuntist, he preferred to work in concise double motives, and the style of his later music draws heavily on the pointed rhythms and clear tonalities—usually major—of the canzonetta. Yet Rore's lessons in the possibilities of chromatic alteration have been thoroughly absorbed and allied with a resource of contrasted vocal scoring which ensured that his colourful madrigals were in constant demand. This is a style of sensuous chiaroscuro, closely related to that of his fellow Venetian, the painter Paolo Veronese. In Andrea Gabrieli, too, we find early traces of the luxuriant style cultivated particularly in Ferrara and Mantua in the last twenty years of the century. But Andrea is still interested in writing for amateurs as well as professionals. He is soon reprinted in northern Europe (though not in England) in collections that are directed towards a bourgeois market, and he is the principal influence on the last and greatest of the madrigalists who still worked within the classical tradition, Luca Marenzio.

Two respected writers on the madrigal, Alfred Einstein and more recently Anthony Newcomb,[11] place Marenzio squarely among the 'virtuosi'. Newcomb particularly emphasizes his contribution to the luxuriant Ferrarese madrigal of the 1580s, with its elaborate written-out ornamentation, runs, roulades and the rest. Now improvised ornamentation was a common enough practice with virtuoso singers and instrumentalists at this time. Towards the end of the century we find an ever-increasing number of pattern books published presumably with the aim of passing on the secrets of embellishment to struggling amateurs.[12] But improvised ornamentation as practised by virtuoso performers was always notably unstructural, concealing rather than enhancing a musical design.[13] It was, in short, anti-classical. Marenzio however treats *fioriture* both in the service of word-painting and of the over-all musical structure. Furthermore, even the most elaborate of Marenzio's written-out *passaggi* are grateful to sing, and seldom beyond the ability of the good amateur. The popularity of his work in northern Europe, and especially in England, proves that. There, trained virtuoso singers were simply not available.[14]

The luxuriant style is associated almost exclusively with two cities, or rather courts, Ferrara and Mantua. Both had notable *ridotti* of female virtuoso singers. From about 1580 onward, the house composers in each centre, Wert and Luzzaschi in Ferrara, Pallavicino and then Monteverdi in Mantua, created a new kind of madrigal for these *concerti delle donne*.[15] Rore's usual five-part texture of soprano, alto, two tenors and bass becomes changed into the brighter sonority of two sopranos, alto, tenor and bass. The emphasis now is on the trio of female voices, and the logical outcome of this concerto-like treatment is the elimination of the male voices altogether, replacing them by a keyboard instrument as in Luzzaschi's *Madrigali per cantare e sonare* of 1601. The disintegration of the classical madrigal by this means is completed by Monteverdi's fifth book of 1605, with its celebration of virtuoso solos accompanied only by instrumental *basso continuo* within the context of madrigals that are still nominally for five voices.

Virtuosity was one of the three threats that I mentioned at the beginning of this paper. Disruption of the polyphonic texture came from two other directions, both of which are in one sense allied to virtuosity, and in another opposed to it. These are affective expressionism and monody.

With the revival of interest in Petrarch in the latter part of the century went the rising star of Tasso and then of Guarini's pastoral play *Il Pastor Fido*. This renewed interest in pathetic texts gave composers ample opportunities to experiment not only with chromaticism, but also with intensified dissonance and the expressive use of formerly forbidden musical intervals. The diminished fourth, for instance, soon became a cliché. The process can be seen very clearly in Giaches de Wert's madrigal books, particularly from his eighth book of 1586 onwards. It is even more obvious in the music of his Mantuan offsider Benedetto Pallavicino. Marenzio himself was not immune from this 'manneristic'[16] fashion. It continues from his sixth book for five voices of 1594 until the crisis of the last two books, the eighth of 1598 and ninth of 1599. Wert never really abandoned the luxuriant style, but already in his seventh and eighth books there are madrigals which rely for their effect on a kind of 'pseudo-monody', a thinly disguised homophonic accompaniment to a top part replete with declamatory, 'affective' intervals and chromatics.[17] In the same way, Marenzio's eighth book of 1598 is almost entirely composed of 'pseudo-monodies', many of them quite short and with little or no text-repetition. Little would be lost in performing them as solo songs, adapting the lower four parts for a continuo instrument. But Marenzio returned to polyphony in his ninth and last book; the final madrigal in it, *La bella man*, even contains a strict canon. The collection as a whole includes some of Marenzio's most anguished and pathetic madrigals as well as some of his most smoothly polished. He is thus not lightly to be coaxed into one particular school. A different case is the Prince of Venosa, Carlo Gesualdo. He was an adherent of the Ferrara school, but in his hands the pathetic, chromatic style is taken to unparalleled lengths and the tonal and polyphonic structure collapses into dissociated incoherence. He is in my opinion the most overrated composer of the late Renaissance.

Why were these composers reaching for such an extreme expressiveness? In the late Renaissance one can detect a shift of emphasis from the Platonic idea of art as 'imitation of nature' towards the Aristotelian idea of catharsis.[18] It was no longer enough to entertain, edify and delight amateurs through their participation in the music. Rather there was a new, passive audience whose affections had to be moved by its emotional involvement in the art of professional performers. The end of this was music drama, and it was significantly through settings of speeches taken from Guarini's tragi-comedy *Il Pastor Fido* that the madrigalists laid the ground for opera itself. Some of these speeches, such as *Cruda Amarilli*, became set pieces in which composers from Wert to Monteverdi could display their command of the new, affective style. Each composer became more extreme than the last, and it is no accident that the shocked conservative Artusi especially noted harmonic licences in Monteverdi's setting of this same speech, *Cruda Amarilli*. The bounds of moderation had been overstepped, and Artusi saw—rightly—the doom of classical polyphony.

It was monody, however, that dealt the final death-blow to the madrigal. Solo song in Italy had in a sense gone underground, but it did survive as a popular performing art, both in the recitation formulae traditionally used for singing stanzas from Ariosto and in the performance of some of the lighter forms, such as the villanesca and villanella. No less a composer than Willaert himself had arranged some of Verdelot's madrigals for solo voice and lute in a print of 1536. And Antonfrancesco Doni, in his *Dialogo della musica* of 1544,[19] writes of amateur performances of madrigals, some sung *a cappella* with one singer to a part, but others sung as solos, accompanied by a lute or viol. There is as well the mid-century fashion for *madrigali ariosi*; these are usually simple, four-part homophonic settings with the melodic interest concentrated in the top part. By about 1575, noted Vincenzo Giustiniani, there were many professional singers famous for their agile voices and skill at improvised embellishment.[20]

But the most important opponent of the classical madrigal attacked it precisely on classical, that is, ancient Greek, authority. Vincenzo Galilei published his *Dialogo della musica antica e della moderna* in Florence in 1581.[21] He had been a pupil and supporter of Zarlino, but his studies in ancient Greek music, aided by a liberal pirating from a correspondence he had exchanged with the Florentine humanist Girolamo Mei, convinced him that the modern madrigal was a corrupt and trivial form of musical art. Its pictorial imagery, he complained, aroused only amusement and even derision, and polyphony could not hope to match notes to the affection of the words, since simultaneous polyphonic lines pulled in different affective ways at once. This was far from ancient Greek accounts of the solo singer being able to move the passions of his audience. In fact, Galilei's attitude towards polyphony was thoroughly ambivalent, and despite his attacks, he never abandoned it himself. His later work included a massive, unpublished treatise on modern counterpoint, in which he advocated new ways of taking dissonances; some of these are strikingly similar to those afterwards employed by Monteverdi.[22] Earlier in his career, Galilei had often preferred to perform favourite madrigals and villanelle to his own lute accompaniment, singing the bass part as a solo, a procedure which seems strangely unmusical, to say the least. In the *Dialogo*, he mentions that he would sing either the bass or the melody, depending on which 'carries the air'.[23] But the qualities he valued above all others in music were simplicity and directness, and he was just as much opposed to the cult of the virtuoso singer as he was to the over-ingenious contrapuntist. He stands therefore in direct line of descent from the frottolists and his citing of classical authority can be read merely as a cover for the re-establishment of a native Italian tradition.

The classical madrigal had been a highly artificial and, in the end, fragile form. Once its polyphonic basis was compromised, it ceased to exist. But it did produce great works of art which still give pleasure today to just the sort of cultivated amateur singers for whom it was originally written. Its only close analogy in the realm of high musical art seems to be the classical Viennese string quartet, another form of music meant to be heard intimately and from within.

Notes

1. Horace, *Satires*, I. i. 106–7.
2. G. M. Artusi, *L'Artusi, ovvero, Delle imperfezioni della moderna musica*, Venice, 1600, trans. O. Strunk, *Source Readings in Music History*, New York, 1950, pp. 393–404.
3. See the articles by C. V. Palisca, 'Artusi, Giovanni Maria', *New Grove Dictionary* (hereafter *NG*), London, 1980, and 'The Artusi-

Monteverdi Controversy', in *The Monteverdi Companion*, ed. D. Arnold and N. Fortune, London, 1968, pp. 133–66.

4. Palisca, 'Artusi', *NG*, i. 647.

5. J. Haar, 'Bembo, Pietro', *NG*, ii. 459.

6. A. Einstein, *The Italian Madrigal*, Princeton, 1971 (2nd edn), i. 206.

7. For a fruitful discussion of the complex relationships between these three, see H. M. Brown, *et al.*, *Chanson and Madrigal, 1480–1530: Studies in Comparison and Contrast (A Conference at Isham Memorial Library, September 13–14, 1961)*, ed. J. Haar, Cambridge, Mass., 1964.

8. See the versions by Franciscus Bossinensis, 1509, printed in B. Disertori, *Le frottole per canto e liuto intabulate de Franciscus Bossinensis*, Milan, 1964.

9. Dare one add the names of Weelkes and Wilbye, extreme *oltremontani* setting Italian music to a foreign tongue? If quantity be ignored in favour of quality, perhaps yes.

10. A. Gardano, Dedication of *Di Cipriano Rore il quinto libro de madrigali a cinque voci*, Venice, 1566 (*RISM* 1566[17]). Facsimile in Rore, *Opera omnia*, ed. B. Meier, Rome 1971, v. p. xix.

11. A. Newcomb, *The Madrigal at Ferrara, 1579–1597*, i (Princeton Studies in Music, vol. vii, 1980), 75–80.

12. See H. M. Brown, *Embellishing Sixteenth-Century Music*, London, 1976.

13. Ibid. p. 34 ('Apparently musicians took pleasure in obscuring the structural elements of a composition, rather than making them as plain as possible').

14. Newcomb, i. 94, cites particularly *Rivi, fontani e fiumi* as 'evidence of Marenzio's continuing cultivation of the luxuriant style at this time', but this madrigal was also published by Phalèse in *Paradiso musicale*, Antwerp, 1596 (*RISM* 1596[10]). Oddly enough, one of Marenzio's most 'luxuriant' madrigals, *Vezzosi augelli*, appeared in his *Madrigali a quattro* (1585), a collection directed to the Roman academies rather than to north Italian *virtuosi*. The unusually wide compass of the tenor —a thirteenth—is curious. A modern edition is in *The Penguin Book of Italian Madrigals for Four Voices*, ed. J. Roche, Harmondsworth, 1974, no. 27.

15. For further information, see Newcomb, *The Madrigal at Ferrara*; I. Fenlon, *Music and Patronage in Sixteenth-Century Mantua*, i (Cambridge Studies in Music, 1980); C. MacClintock, *Giaches de Wert (1535–1596): Life and Works* (Musicological Studies and Documents, vol. xvii, 1966); D. Arnold, *Monteverdi* (2nd rev. edn), London, 1975; K. Bosi Monteath, 'The Five-Part Madrigals of Benedetto Pallavicino', unpublished Ph.D. dissertation, University of Otago, N.Z., 1981.

16. 'Mannerism', a term fashionably applied nowadays to madrigals of this type, is still too controversial a style label to be generally useful. For a fascinating discussion (with which I do not wholly agree) of the topic in relation to late Renaissance musical style, see M. R. Maniates, *Mannerism in Italian Music and Culture, 1530–1630*, Chapel Hill, 1979.

17. *Misera, non credea* from the eighth book of 1586, is a good example. See Giaches de Wert, *Collected Works*, ed. C. MacClintock and M. Bernstein, viii, [Rome?], 1968, no. 8.

18. Cf. B. R. Hanning, *Of Poetry and Music's Power: Humanism and the Creation of Opera*, Ann Arbor, 1969, p. 8: ('For Zarlino, for example, it was obvious that modern music did not produce the same results as ancient; but he attributed this discrepancy to the different aims of contemporary music which sought to dispose its listeners to virtue, and, in delighting, to instruct them. This view, based on Platonic and Horatian theories of art, remained in contrast to the newly fashionable Aristotelian concept of moving the hearers to various emotions in order to purge them of these emotions').

19. *RISM* 1544[22].

20. V. Giustiniani, *Discorso sopra la musica*, c. 1628, trans, C. MacClintock, [Rome?], 1962, p. 68.

21. Facsimile reprint, New York, 1967; relevant sections in English translation by O. Strunk, *Source Readings in Music History*, pp. 302–22.

22. C. V. Palisca, 'Vincenzo Galilei's Counterpoint Treatise: A Code for the *Seconda pratica*', *Journal of the American Musicological Society*, ix (1956), 81.

23. C. V. Palisca, 'Vincenzo Galilei and Some Links Between "Pseudo-Monody" and Monody', *Musical Quarterly*, xlvi (1960), 344–60.

3

Passion, Imagination, and Intellect:
Poussin, Claude, and Gaspard Dughet in the Roman Campagna

P. A. Tomory

I intend to take the general title of this symposium literally. It was the classical tempering of passion, imagination, and intellect in the works of these three artists, Poussin, Claude, and Gaspard Dughet, which led to the maturation of the aesthetic response to a particular landscape and its variety of associations which we still experience today.

I would stress 'maturation', for the painting of landscape with sentient expression both of its phenomena and the emotions stirred by them was pioneered by Northern and Venetian artists around 1500, and continued by both throughout the sixteenth century. It was to the Venetians, particularly Titian and his followers, that Annibale and Agostino Carracci in Bologna owed their first inclination to turn their acute observation of everyday life to that of nature in the late 1580s. By the beginning of the seventeenth century Annibale had laid the foundations of the art of painting landscape, that is of providing those figure subjects that required it with a convincing natural context, which not only purveyed a sense of 'actuality' of place and time but the human mood appropriate to the subject. While Annibale did not accomplish this unaided, it was he who initiated the concept of the so-called 'ideal' landscape. This concept was then extended in terms of variety by Domenichino and others and brought to maturity, as I have said, by Poussin, Claude, and Dughet.

Before proceeding, there is one aspect of painting that requires notice, namely the expression of form, whether it be 'solid' or 'nebulous' like air or cloud. In the fifteenth century artists generally employed only a 'visual' representation of form, but in the sixteenth century the Venetian artists added 'tactile' characterizations. Thus form was not only represented as it looked but how it felt, this being accomplished by variations in paint texture and other techniques. This additional sense element is as fundamental to a convincing creation of natural surroundings and atmosphere by the painter as similar components are to the poet and the composer.

However, this innovation of the Venetian artists could hardly have taken place without the presence of a more widespread shift in human cognition from what we might term 'single sense definition' to one composed of two or more senses. Obviously the complex reasons for this change cannot be discussed here, but the account that follows should make the significance of this shift clear.

There can be no individual empathy with nature without recourse to the senses, but in the first half of the sixteenth century the senses were still judged to unleash base passions unless they were controlled by holy reason. This a print of Baccio Bandinelli's allegory *Battle between Reason and the Senses* shows very well. There Venus, Cupid, and Vulcan representing Passion, and Apollo, Diana, Hercules, and others representing Virtue, oppose each other, while in the sky Reason sheds light on the side of Virtue and dense clouds on Passion; an inscribed couplet on the engraving may be translated as follows: 'O mortals learn that the stars are as superior to clouds as Holy Reason is to base desires.'[1]

In the same decade, however, Ignatius Loyola, founder of the Jesuits, published his *Spiritual Exercises* (1548) in which the exercitant was instructed to imagine the affliction of the senses in Hell (Meditation 12) and the exaltation of the senses in Heaven (Meditation 20). Indeed, the emphasis in the Exercises is on the self-induction of sensory experiences through spiritual fervour. Then in 1563 Lambinus published his authoritative edition of Lucretius's *De Rerum Natura* ('The Nature of the Universe') which was to remain the standard text until Lachmann's in 1850.[2] In Book IV, Lucretius, who wrote his poem in the first century B.C., discusses the senses in detail, providing the antithesis to that illustrated in Bandinelli's allegory; how could reason prevail against the senses, 'being itself wholly derived from the senses'?[3] Almost in the same year (in 1561) Frans Floris's series of the Five Senses was engraved by Cornelius Cort, then resident in Italy, but followed shortly after by another series, designed by Marten de Vos and engraved by Adrian Collaert, in which Floris's single figures and their attributes were provided with background references to Adam and Eve and Christ to illustrate the genesis of the senses and their continuing spiritual associations.[4] This latter series can be seen as providing a reconciliation between sacred and profane; for the central images are wholly profane since they are directly related to the *Four Temperaments*—Sanguine, Choleric, Melancholic, Phlegmatic—correlated by Antiochus of Athens in the second century with the signs of the Zodiac, the four elements, the four ages of man and, importantly for this study, the four seasons.[5]

As an example, *Sight* (Fig. 7) shares with the Choleric temperament an eagle, emblematic in the former of its keen sight and in the latter of the all-seeing eye of Zeus or Jupiter, which may be seen in the set of Temperaments engraved by Virgile Solis of Nuremburg.[6] These conjunctions of Antiochus are clearly illustrated by Francesco Albani in his ceiling painting of *c.* 1616 in the Palazzo Verospi, Rome, engraved by Frezza (Fig. 8).[7] In the centre, Apollo as the Sun encircled by the Zodiac controls the Seasons, Venus/Spring, Ceres/Summer, Bacchus/Autumn, Vulcan/ Winter. To the left there is Dusk and Night, and to the right Dawn and Day. In the spandrels, from top left there are the planets, Mars, Jupiter (with Juno), Saturn; from bottom left Venus, Mercury, and the Moon. Then in reverse order Monday to Saturday. Although Albani drew his emblematic imagery from Cesare Ripa's *Iconologia*,[8] the dominant source of the seventeenth century, this ceiling effectively synthesizes the universal controls of temporal life established in Antiquity.

The correlation between these controls and the individual temperament can be very well demonstrated in Claude's painting *Psyche and the Palace of Love* (Fig. 9), its textual source being Apuleius's *Metamorphoses* (IV–V) in which the story of Cupid and Psyche is related.[9] Psyche is here distraught pending the revelation of her immortal lover. The time of day is dusk and the season late autumn controlled by Jupiter and Saturn, indicated by the two elements Earth and Water, which are also represented in Virgile Solis's engraving of *Melancholy* where Melancholia sits like Psyche, accompanied by a stag which loves solitude, and by a Swan, which sings a melancholy song before it dies and is also an emblem of love.[10] Both stag and swans can be seen in the middle ground of Claude's painting. Evident here is the recognized coupling of temperaments—melancholic/phlegmatic—for Psyche, deprived of mortal love, is resigned to the fate predicted for her by Apollo.

Furthermore the stag, because of its keen hearing, is also an emblem of the sense of sound, and (as Apuleius relates) after Psyche sights the castle she enters it, where a disembodied voice urges her to refresh herself by tasting the wines and meats, to the unseen accompaniment of a singer and a harp. Finally, when she is in bed, her unknown lover comes to touch her for the first time.

This sequence of sensory experiences is followed almost exactly by Giambattista Marino in his long, florid, and erotic poem *L'Adone*, published in 1623.[11] For in Cantos VI to VIII he tells how Adonis is guided through the gardens of the senses, but interpolates near-clinical descriptions of the sense organs—the Eye and Nose (Canto VI), the Ear and Mouth (Canto VII)—which are elaborations of those given by Lucretius in his *De Rerum Natura*.[12] The last garden is that of Touch or *Pleasure and Wantoness*, for there Adonis is united with Venus. That the senses and temperaments are depicted in the open air with the attendant fauna and flora of nature is, of course, to indicate their universal and eternal character, a spaceless and timeless context which might satisfy the natural philosopher, but for individual human experience, like Psyche's, place and time are essential requirements. But whereas time may be past, present, or future, place must be fixed, for human recollection or imagination requires such an anchor to swing about in the tides of the senses. This Cicero implied in his *De Finibus Bonorum et Malorum*: 'Whether it is a natural instinct or a mere illusion, I can't say; but one's emotions are more strongly aroused by seeing the places that tradition records to have been the favourite resort of men of note in former days, than by hearing about their deeds or reading their writings.'[13]

For the three artists of this study the Roman Campagna was the place that so strongly aroused their emotions. For Gaspard Dughet, born of French parents in Rome, this was the only landscape he was ever to know, while for his brother-in-law Poussin and Claude, both French expatriates, it was to be the landscape in which they were to spend the greatest part of their working lives. Nor did they dream their visions of the Campagna's associations with the antique past in their studios, but on horseback or on foot, visiting regularly those localities most redolent of that past.[14] Thus for instance we can share the artist's actual experience of the panorama in Gaspard Dughet's *The Roman Campagna* (National Gallery, London) or the roadway vista in Poussin's *View in the Campagna* (National Gallery, London). A frequently quoted excursion is that recorded by the German artist Sandrart when he was in Rome (1629–35), 'Another time Poussin, Claude Lorrain, [Van Laer] and I were riding out to Tivoli to paint or draw landscape';[15] in German he wrote *Landschaften nach dem Leben* ('landscape from life'); it was, then, with these topographical particulars that these artists constructed their imaginative landscapes of antiquity. Only with sensory experiences of actuality seeded in the imagery can the spectator have his own senses respond or his emotions stirred.

No place in the Campagna had more associations or a more spectacular setting than Tivoli, the Roman Tibur. Julius Caesar, Mark Antony, Augustus, and Hadrian all lived there, and the poets Virgil, Juvenal, Propertius, and Horace praised its attractions.[16] Its associations with prehistory were also famous for it had a rich temple dedicated to Hercules, and the Tiburtine Sibyl boomed out her oracle from a grotto by the Anio waterfall, Tivoli's best known natural feature. This waterfall, as Goethe might have described it, is *der Ur-Wasserfall*, the original waterfall of our picturesque vocabulary, and it features in this painting by Gaspard Dughet (Fig. 10), with the so-called Temple of the Sibyl on the hill crest. Although this is not a painting done 'on the spot' its sense of 'actuality' is distilled from the artist's drawings, made not as preparatory sketches for the painting, but as immediate sense responses to place and time.[17]

There is little wonder, then, that Horace, who had a villa at Tivoli and later a farm nearby in the Sabine hills, could write,

> But as for me, neither the sturdy Spartan
> Hills nor the lush low fields of Larissa can knock at the heart as
> My Tibur does, the Sibyl's booming grotto,
> Anio's fine cascade, Tiburnus' grove and the orchards
> Whose rivulets weave a dance of irrigation,[18]

and describe or imply in just five lines of verse the experiences of all five senses.

That the senses were recognized at the time, with the prompting of Lucretius, as the primal sources of the knowledge of both pleasure and pain, is evidenced by these artists' fascination with primeval nature and its mythic inhabitants, as, for example, in Poussin's *Landscape with Polyphemus* (Fig. 11), inspired by Ovid's *Metamorphoses* XIII. But Philostratus tells us in his *Imagines* that the land of the Cyclops produces its fruits spontaneously without cultivation; that the Cyclops are cannibals and live in the clefts of mountains.[19] This is in accord with Lucretius's description of early man as a denizen of 'the woods and forests and mountain caves', and the satyr who is about to leap on the nymphs on the right in Poussin's painting graphically illustrates the poet's observations that since there were no rules of marriage or behaviour 'woman was attracted by mutual desire, or caught by the man's violent force and vehement lust'.[20] But Polyphemus on the mountain top is in love with the sea nymph Galatea and plays on his pipes some elemental melody. Love, even in primitive times, is thus seen as a gentling force and the sound of music its sense accompaniment.

In Poussin's day, music may also have 'soothed the savage breast' but it was also considered as a prime agent in the seduction of young women.[21] The painting thus hints, perhaps, at the corruptive influence of civilization. The succeeding mythological age is interpreted by Claude in his *Apollo and the Muses* (Fig. 12), where nature, the elemental stimulus of the senses, nurtures the creative arts in its solitude. As Horace wrote in one of his letters: 'The whole chorus of poets loves the grove and flees the town.'[22] Here the presence of swans and a stag point to the Melancholic temperament, the temperament of the creative artist who works alone.[23] The swan is also an attribute of Apollo and the Muses.[24] The river god, as *genius loci*, marks the landscape as an ancient one but the distant mountain specifies the Campagna, for this is, surely, Soracte, on whose summit there once stood a temple to Apollo, who was described by Virgil as 'greatest of gods, guardian of sacred Soracte!' But when 'Soracte stands glistening in its mantle of snow . . . and the streams are frozen with the biting cold' Horace calls for more wood on the fire and a jar of four-year-old Sabine wine; not even the Muse stirs in winter![25] It was also Horace who provided the imaginative dictum of this century, *Ut pictura poesis*.[26] Poetry is like a painting, which these artists reversed to paint poetic visions, believing the poet when he wrote: 'Bacchus I saw on distant crags—believe me, ye of after time—teaching hymns, and I beheld the nymphs his pupils, and the goat-footed satyrs . . . My heart thrills with fear . . . and tumultuously rejoices.'[27]

Poussin seems to have seen this too in *The Andrians* (Fig. 13) through the description of Philostratus of an ancient painting, 'For by act of Dionysus the earth of the Andrians is so charged with wine that it bursts forth and sends up for them a river. . . . The men, crowned with ivy and bryony, are singing . . . that this river . . . is a draught drawn from Dionysus. . . . This is what you should imagine you hear.'[28] And this is what we see in the autumnal evening light. Dusk, as one saw in Albani's ceiling, flits like the bat between Day and Night—a crepuscular metamorphosis of time and the poet-painter's fleeting vision, his senses tuned momentarily to the sight, the sound, the taste, the smell, and the touch of fertile pleasures long past. A far less gentle and noisier revelry is present in Poussin's *Triumph of Pan* (Morison Collection: Sudeley Castle) for as Philostratus again explained, 'Pan, the nymphs say, dances badly and goes beyond bounds in his leaping'[29]—a true Choleric, impetuous and aggressive, Pan is the source of panic fear and the nightmare. Poussin's colours in this painting are appropriately summer bright for that is the season of the Choleric but the time is late afternoon for at high noon Pan was at his most dangerous; then he slept, and if disturbed his nostrils would flare with anger—the quiet before the storm! But Philostratus also tells us 'that when Pindar began to write poetry, Pan neglected his leaping and sang the Odes of Pindar'.[30] Bacchus is thus fertile nature, Pan chaotic nature, or, expressed in literary terms, the wild leaps of the imagination have to be cultivated to produce poetic fruit. We are reminded that creativity, like love, is a climactic synthesis of pleasure and pain.

It is, however, a climatic synthesis that attends Dughet's *Union of Aeneas and Dido* (Fig. 14). Virgil tells the story of Juno, in the company of Venus, Aeneas's mother, creating the storm—'a confused rumbling started in the sky. Then came the rain clouds and the showers mixed with hail. . . . The lightning flared'; which forces Aeneas and Dido, who are out hunting, to take shelter in a cave where they effect their union. Virgil concludes his account with, 'On that day were sown the seeds of suffering and death';[31] for Aeneas is to desert Dido and she will commit suicide. Venus is not only the Goddess of Love, but the planet controlling the season of Spring, and it is in the Spring, as Lucretius recounts, that 'the temperature of the sky is set between the two [cold and heat], then all the different causes of the thunderbolt are combined. For the choppy currents of the year mingle cold and heat. . . . It is no wonder if at that time very many thunderbolts are made, and a turbulent tempest is stirred up in the sky'.[32] In the painting a strike of lightning has shorn a limb off the tree in the foreground, which Lucretius describes in another passage: 'We hear the thunder after the eyes see the lightning, [for] . . . things always take longer to reach the ears than [the eyes]'; and on the sky

> the winds carry clouds like mountains across through the air . . . you will . . . recognize the great masses of them, and . . . perceive the similitude of caverns reared with vaulted roofs, which . . . the winds fill, and with loud roaring resent their imprisonment . . . roaming round in quest of a way out, and rolling together the seeds of fire . . . send the flame rushing about the hollow furnaces within, until they have shattered the cloud and flashed forth coruscating.[33]

So, also, is the storm of passion, or the poetic frenzy.

If the senses, however, are the primary sources of experience, reason is the synthesizer and arbiter. For what we have seen so far is, on the one hand, the ennobling of landscape, through associations with ancient mythology, literature, and thought, the elevation of it from its purely topographic or its 'background' roles and, on the other, the involvement of the spectator in this 'ennobling' process, through the striking of responses from his senses and thence his intellect. While the artist's reason synthesizes his actual sense experiences it also arbitrates the form and presentation of the 'idea' that grows from them.[34] In effect, the spectator has to be placed in a metamorphic position between fact—his real experiences—and the transcendent illusion of the artist's sentient imagery.

All this may be demonstrated in Poussin's *Landscape with Diogenes* (Fig. 15), which refers to how Diogenes, seeing a peasant scoop up water in his hand, throws away his drinking cup. The senses of sight and taste are immediately evoked, but it is reason that arbitrates whether a hand is a satisfactory replacement for a cup. This reasoning of Diogenes is directed by his anti-materialistic philosophy. He had even fled from the city to live in a barrel in the country. Through association, however, one is reminded of Horace writing to his friend Fuscus: 'Is the water purer which in city-streets struggles to burst its leaden pipes than that which dances and purls adown the sloping brook?'; and elsewhere, 'Why should I change my Sabine dale for the greater burden of wealth?'[35]

Thus the freedom and the enjoyment of simple pleasures, which we still find in country life, are 'ennobled' through philosophic and poetic example. Since Diogenes, as founder of the Cynics, was claimed by the Stoics as a philosophic progenitor and Poussin espoused Stoicism, the artist becomes the spectator's *alter ego* in the same metamorphic space between reality and illusion.

That Nature, imperfect though it is, is the only continuum in mortal life, is expressed in Claude's painting *Landscape with the Arch of Constantine* (Fig. 16), which may well have been inspired by a Latin poem by Urban VIII on the ruins of ancient Rome and their representation of the transitoriness of earthly things.[36] *Sic transit gloria mundi*, as Lucretius implied: 'Do you not see that even stones are conquered by time, that tall turrets fall and rocks crumble, that the gods' temples . . . wear out and crack? . . . Do we not see the monuments of men fall to pieces?'[37] But Claude, even if he knew of these literary sources, would have actually seen peasants driving their cattle through the Arch of Constantine, close by the Colosseum, to let them graze on the Campo Vaccino, once the mighty Forum of ancient Rome, and in the golden light of the sunset envision this metamorphosis of imperial architecture to the natural matter from which it was constructed.

In this paper, the discussion has proceeded from 'passion', the seventeenth-century term for feeling, through imagination, to intellect, for that is the artistic order of creation, particularly as regards landscape and the ennobling process, which was to promote it as a subject in its own right. Since all secular subjects, apart from those of portraiture and genre, had to be justified in some way by classical reference, then the landscapists had to do likewise. In the case of Lucretius's *De Rerum Natura*, they were presented with a text book written with great feeling and urgency, which gave them, in detail, the scientific descriptions and explanations of the human and natural phenomena that they needed to synthesize with, say, an imaginative episode from Virgil or a poetic response by Horace to his natural environment.[38]

However, these last comments should not be taken to suggest that these artists were but inspired illustrators of classical poetic texts. Their paintings are adequate proof that none of them was painting anything else but his own conception of the natural environment. That this natural environment had been 'ennobled' by ancient and familiar mythological, historical and poetic associations was a vital factor in enabling the paintings of these artists to transcend the normal limitations to the appeal of any given regional locality, and to communicate to the educated European at large the evocative powers of the forms and phenomena of nature. I can conclude, therefore, by rephrasing Cicero's observation that I quoted earlier: These artists were enabled to arouse both emotional and intellectual responses by the classical tempering of natural instinct and mere illusion.

Notes

1. Bandinelli's allegory was engraved by Nicolas Béatrizet (Bartsch 44) and dated 1545. See J. Seznec, *The Survival of the Pagan Gods*, New York, 1953, pp. 110–2, n. 112, and fig. 38; E. Panofsky, *Studies in Iconology*, New York, 1939, pp. 149–50, n. 70.

2. Lambinus's edition was published in Paris. But Lucretius was known in the late fifteenth century; cf. Panofsky, pp. 63 ff.

3. *De Rerum Natura*, ed. W. H. D. Rouse (Loeb edn), London, 1924, 1975 repr., p. 315 (IV. 483–4).

4. C. van de Velde, *Frans Floris*, Brussels, 1975, i. 431–2, ii. figs. 288–92: the set designed by Marten de Vos, engraved by Adrian Collaert (Hollstein, 437–40). Fig. 7 reproduces *Sight* from a reversed series of *c.* 1600, by an anonymous Netherlands engraver after the de Vos set, which points to the popularity of this series.

5. See Seznec, pp. 45, 47.

6. *The Four Temperaments* (Bartsch 178–81). This set has been dated 1550–5; see I. O'Dell-Franke, *Kupferstiche und Radierung aus der Werkstatt des Virgil Solis*, Wiesbaden, 1977, p. 66, cat. nos. and figs. e67–e70.

7. For Albani, H. Bodmer, 'Die Fresken des Francesco Albani in Palazzo Verospi zu Rom', *Pantheon*, xviii (1936), 366–9, is still the most reliable account. The Palazzo Verospi is now the Credito Italiano bank in the Corso, Rome.

8. C. Ripa, *Iconologia*, 1603 edn, Temperaments 75–80; The Seasons, 473–7; Times of Day, Dawn/Evening, 95–7, Day (Aurora), 60, Night 360–1; The Senses 447–9.

9. *Metamorphoses (The Golden Ass)*, ed. S. Gaselee (Loeb edn), London, 1915, 1977 repr., pp. 199 ff. M. Kitson, *The Art of Claude Lorrain*, London, 1969, Cat. No. 34, supposes the scene to be after Psyche's union with Cupid but she was also distraught *before* her meeting with Cupid.

10. See G. de Tervarent, *Attributs et Symboles dans L'Art Profane 1450–1600*, Geneva, 1958, pp. 67, 140.

11. Marino was in Paris from 1615 to 1623 when he met Poussin and encouraged him to go to Italy, where he also introduced him to

patrons in Rome; see F. Haskell, *Patrons and Painters*, London, 1980 (2nd edn), pp. 38, 44. The drawings at Windsor by Poussin once thought to be of subjects from *L'Adone* are probably from Ovid's *Metamorphoses*; see C. Pace, *Felibien's Life of Poussin*, London, 1981, p. 151, n. 9.5.

12. Lucretius's descriptions of the sense organs are based on the atomic theory advanced much earlier by Democritus and his successor Epicurus.

13. *De Finibus Bonorum et Malorum*, ed. H. Rackham (Loeb edn), London, 1914, 1971 repr., p. 391 (V. i. 2).

14. Two maps of the Campagna were available to these artists: Fabio Magini, *Campagna di Roma olim Latium*, Bologna, 1620, and Joannes Blaeu, *Campagna di Roma...*, Amsterdam, 1647. The latter was dedicated to Cassiano del Pozzo, the influential patron of Poussin.

15. Joachim von Sandrart, *Academie de Bau-Bild-Mahlerey-Kunsten*, ed. A. R. Peltzer, 1925, p. 184. Sandrart, like Solis, from Nuremburg, probably introduced Claude to the Solis series of the Temperaments which are in fact more 'poetic' than those of Ripa.

16. On Horace and Tivoli see Gilbert Highet, *Poets in a Landscape*, New York, 1957, ch. IV.

17. In a passage on working from nature Sandrart observes, 'This is in my opinion the best manner to impress the truth precisely on the mind: because body and soul are as it were brought together in it'; quoted by M. Röthlisberger, *Claude Lorrain: the Paintings*, New Haven, 1961, i. 51.

18. *The Odes of Horace*, trans. James Michie (Penguin Classics), Harmondsworth, 1967, p. 31 (I. vii).

19. *Imagines*, ed. A. Fairbanks (Loeb edn), London, 1931, 1969 repr., II. 18.

20. *De Rerum Natura*, p. 453 (V. 955–65).

21. Poussin was deeply interested in music and was introduced to G. Zarlino's *Instituzione Harmoniche* by Domenichino in 1634. For music and seduction see Salvator Rosa's Satire *Music* composed in 1640.

22. *Satires, Epistles and Ars Poetica*, ed. H. R. Fairclough (Loeb edn), London, 1926, 1978 repr., p. 431 (*Ep.* II. ii. 77). This reference was also quoted by Ripa in his entry on *Melancholia*.

23. For the creative artist and Melancholia see R. Klibansky, E. Panofsky and F. Saxl, *Saturn and Melancholy*, London, 1964.

24. Cf. Tervarent, op. cit. Horace (*Odes*, II. xx) describes how he imagines himself metamorphosing into a swan, an intimation of his immortality.

25. Virgil, *Aeneid*, ed. H. R. Fairclough (Loeb edn), London, 1918, 1967 repr., ii. 289 (XI. 785). Horace, *The Odes and Epodes*, ed. C. E.

Bennett (Loeb edn), London, 1914, 1978 repr., p. 29 (*Odes*, I. ix). Mte Soracte or Soratte (2267 feet) is approximately 26 miles north of Rome near Civita Castellana. Travellers in the seventeenth century knew that it marked one day's journey to Rome. Soracte has been identified in Gaspard Dughet's *Landscape with Armida and Rinaldo* Palazzo Corsini, (Inv. 386), see *Paesisti e Vedutisti a Roma nel'600 e nel'700*, Rome, 1956.

26. *Satires, Epistles and Ars Poetica*, p. 480 (*Ars Poetica*, 1. 361).

27. *Odes and Epodes*, p. 161 (*Odes*, II. xix).

28. *Imagines*, pp. 97, 99 (I. 25).

29. Ibid. p. 177 (II. 11).

30. Ibid. p. 181 (II. 12). Cf. Salvator Rosa's *Pindar and Pan*, Chigi Collection, Ariccia; see L. Salerno, *L'Opera completa di Salvator Rosa*, Milan, 1975, No. 208.

31. *Aeneid*, i. 406 (IV. 169–70).

32. *De Rerum Natura*, p. 521 (VI 357–78).

33. Ibid. pp. 505 ff. (VI. 160–6, 189–203).

34. See G. P. Bellori, *Le Vite de' Pittori, Scultori et Architetti Moderni*, Rome, 1672, pp. 3–13.

35. *Satires, Epistles and Ars Poetica*, p. 317 (*Ep.* I. x. 20–1); *Odes and Epodes*, p. 173 (*Odes*, III. i. 47–8).

36. See L. Pastor, *History of the Popes from the Close of the Middle Ages*, London, 1938–53, 6th edn, xxix. 416; *Opere scelte del conte Fulvio Testi*, Modena, 1817, ii. 59.

37. *De Rerum Natura*, p. 403 (V. 306–11).

38. Coincidental with this painterly interest there was a mounting interest in philosophic and scientific circles, e.g. J. C. Magnen's edition of the life and philosophy of Democritus, Ticino, 1646 and Pierre Gassendi's edition and commentary of the writings of Epicurus, Paris, 1649. In 1657 the Accademia del Cimento was founded in Florence to pursue experimental science.

4

The Tensions of Classicism in the French Theatre of the Seventeenth Century

Elliott Forsyth

There is a common belief in English-speaking countries that French classicism was essentially preoccupied with matters of artistic form, which it sought to regulate by means of rules derived from the Ancients, who were seen as having attained the ultimate in the search for beauty and the portrayal of human nature. This view is summed up, with a characteristic touch of irony, by Alexander Pope in his *Essay on Criticism* (ll. 713–18):

> The *Rules*, a Nation born to serve, obeys,
> And *Boileau* still in Right of *Horace* sways.
> But *we*, brave *Britons*, *Foreign Laws* despis'd,
> And kept *unconquer'd*, and *unciviliz'd*,
> Fierce for the *Liberties of Wit*, and bold,
> We still defy'd the *Romans*, as *of old*.

It is true that much literary debate of the classical age in France focused on questions of form and compliance with rules, and it is true that Boileau, summing them up in his *Art poétique* (to which Pope owed much), makes considerable use of Horace; but it is difficult to imagine that the major literary works of the classical period could have been held in such high esteem in many parts of Europe for a hundred years or more solely on the basis of criteria of this kind. We are thus led to ask whether the content of the great works pushes these formal requirements into the background or whether the great writers make some more constructive use of the rules. Since so many of the literary debates of the time were centred on the theatre, I propose to examine certain aspects of the relationship between form and content in the French theatre of the seventeenth century; and especially the tensions that exist between them in the works of the major dramatists, in an attempt to show something of the nature of the classical temper in France.

But first of all, let us be clear about our terms. In France, the words 'classical' and 'classicism' are used primarily to designate the literature and other arts of a type dominant in the seventeenth century, particularly during the reign of Louis XIV. While some critics limit the strictly classical period in literature to the central part of Louis's reign (1660–1685), it seems more appropriate to place the starting-point some twenty years earlier, in about 1640, at the end of the reign of Louis XIII, when Corneille was writing his most important plays against a background of classical theory and evolving dramatic forms which had been taking shape well before this.

During this central part of the seventeenth century, we are told, the classical rules had a special place. In fact the so-called 'rules' were only elements in a structured theory, whose nature and requirements are set out, with varying emphases, in a considerable number of works written between the sixteenth and eighteenth centuries.[1]

The main sources of these ideas were the ancient writers Aristotle and Horace. But the main sources were not necessarily tapped directly: in France, in the first half of the seventeenth century, when the knowledge of Greek acquired during the Renaissance had largely been lost, the writings of Aristotle were known mainly through Latin translations (generally glossed) and the commentaries of Italian scholars, channels which produced an interesting variety of interpretations. At the practical level, the doctrine was interpreted to a large extent through the Latin models inherited from Antiquity.

From this body of ideas and models, the French theorists derived four main principles. Firstly, following Horace, they declared that all art should have a *moral purpose* made more acceptable by an entertaining presentation. The sixteenth-century Italian theorist Scaligero, whose influence in France was considerable, had summed up the double aim of aesthetic pleasure and moral instruction in the phrase *docere cum delectatione*. There were dissenting voices, but this principle ran deep in the stream of classical theory. Secondly, the work of art must be based on *reason* (as opposed to fantasy and imagination), which guides the poet's genius and dictates his precepts. Thirdly, art must essentially be the *imitation of nature*, but we need to be aware that, for the classical writers, the term 'nature' meant primarily human nature. Finally, the finest art mingled the personal element with the imitation of the Ancients.

It's within the context of these general principles that we must see the classical rules. Of these, the ones most relevant to the theatre are *la vraisemblance*, the rule of verisimilitude; *les bienséances*, the rule of decorum, which called for internal harmony and proprieties; the rule of the *distinction of genres*, which forbade, for example, the mixing of tragic and comic elements in the same work; and lastly, the celebrated rule of the *three unities*: the unities of action, time and place. There were also rules about the main dramatic genres, and the seventeenth-century theorists, moving away from the concept of tragedy as an elegiac form, as it had tended to be during the Renaissance, saw increasingly the importance of the concentration of the action, and urged that the play begin near the climax of the drama (*in medias res*), interest being maintained by the use of suspense. Comedy was governed by few specific rules, except that its characters were to be ordinary people rather than people of noble condition, and its subject-matter was to be about everyday life and invented rather than of historical importance. Otherwise, the general rules of tragedy applied.

How then were these principles and rules applied by the major French dramatists? Is there evidence of conflict between theory and practice? Did the demands of the theorists hinder the work of the artists?

In attempting to answer these questions, we need to be aware, first of all, that the theory was not a single, monolithic block, for there was much debate about interpretation. Then too, we must be aware that the dramatists themselves were to some extent theorists and thus contributed, on the basis of their practical experience, to the development and interpretation of the theory. Finally, we should note that the more acrimonious debates between writers and critics were often stirred up by non-literary factors.

This latter point is especially true of the great comic writer and actor of the French classical theatre, Molière. The last fifteen years of Molière's life, during which he produced all his major comedies and performed frequently at the court of Louis XIV, were spent in an atmosphere of unrelenting controversy through the attacks of critics, rivals and pietists as well as those who saw themselves as victims of his satire.

The first of Molière's major comedies, *L'Ecole des Femmes*, was initially performed in 1662 with immense success, but it touched off immediately a series of virulent attacks. The play is concerned with the question of the education of women and ridicules those men who seek to promote marital security by bringing up girls in a sequestered environment, ignorant of the temptations of this world. Molière was accused by the devout and prudish alike of impiety, immorality and even obscenity (the word *obscénité* being a neologism at the time) on account of scenes which were deemed to mock religion or in which the comic effect turned on verbal ambiguity. Such features were considered to be infringements of the rule of the proprieties, and he was accused by critics and rivals of poor techniques of construction, incoherent characterization and vulgarity. But the play continued to attract an audience, and Molière wrote a short comic piece to accompany it, *La Critique de L'Ecole des Femmes*, in which he answers his detractors.

We might be tempted to think, from some of the comments made in the *Critique* and in other polemical writings, that Molière rejected the classical rules, which by this time were well established: in fact, he considers them as simple observations prompted by good sense and wholly dependent on the ultimate rule, which is to please the public:

> DORANTE: Il semble, à vous ouïr parler, que ces règles de l'art soient les plus grands mystères du monde; et cependant ce ne sont que quelques observations aisées, que le bon sens a faites sur ce qui peut ôter le plaisir que l'on prend à ces sortes de poèmes; et le même bon sens qui a fait autrefois ces observations les fait aisément tous les jours sans le secours d'Horace et d'Aristote. Je voudrais bien savoir si la grande règle de toutes les règles n'est pas de plaire, et si une pièce de théâtre qui a attrapé son but n'a pas suivi un bon chemin.[2]

In other words, the rules are seen as a means of achieving successful drama rather than as a criterion for judgement.

But the principle of pleasing the public is not merely a pretext for pandering to a crude popular taste. In various places, Molière proclaims that comedy has a moral purpose, thus following the fundamental principle of classical art derived by the theorists from Horace. In a letter to the King about his highly controversial comedy *Tartuffe*, he begins:

> Le devoir de la comédie étant de corriger les hommes en les divertissant, j'ai cru que, dans l'emploi où je me trouve, je n'avais rien de mieux à faire que d'attaquer par des peintures ridicules les vices de mon siècle.[3]

Molière's claim of a moral purpose has been contested during the last thirty years or so by critics who take the view that he was primarily concerned to exploit subjects that make good theatre. This is a question which calls for more extensive debate than is possible here. Suffice it to say, in the words of one of these critics, the late Will Moore, that, implicit in Molière's pictures of misanthrope, miser and hypochondriac is at least 'a critique of the modern world'.[4]

But what other classical elements do we find in his plays? If we look at the structure of his major comedies, particularly the *comédies de caractère*, we see that, even though the basic plot follows the pattern of a traditional comedy of intrigue, Molière builds his play according to classical principles of progression, using, for example a unified action within a limited time span in such a way as to produce a more powerful effect through concentration than would be possible with a complicated comic imbroglio. An analysis of individual scenes shows within them a masterly concern with form in matters of symmetry and dramatic progression as well as language. While the principle of verisimilitude (*vraisemblance*) may, to our modern minds, be strained by unlikely *dénouements* dictated to a large extent by theatrical tradition, he manages to create central characters in whom there is a judicious balance of caricature and authenticity. And whatever his critics and enemies may have said about verbal ambiguities and his views on religion, there is much more respect for the proprieties in Molière's comedies than in the ancient theatre and the traditional French and Italian farce which were his main sources.[5]

But the greatness of Molière does not, of course, merely depend on his mastery of the rules; it lies rather in his capacity to observe human behaviour with all its frailties, and to use traditions, literary sources, rules and stage techniques acquired over many years of theatrical experience to achieve a rich and critical portrayal of human nature.

This creative tension evident in the comedies of Molière is perhaps more apparent in the field of tragedy, which in many ways epitomizes the classical ideal.

When Pierre Corneille, in 1640, presented the first French tragedy generally recognized as classical, *Horace*, he was already responding to bitter criticism of his earlier work proffered in the name of classical doctrine. At this time, twenty years before Molière produced his first major comedies, tragedy modelled on the works of antiquity had been written and produced in France for nearly ninety years.[6] A significant professional theatre had however been active for only about thirty years of that time. In the early part of the century, alongside humanist tragedies in the Renaissance style, the French theatre had seen some of the excesses of baroque tragedy, a kind of tragedy of blood reminiscent of the Elizabethan stage, often crude in style and construction but characterised by dynamic action. But tragedy had virtually died in France in the 1620s, being supplanted in the theatre by tragi-comedy, and its rebirth had taken place quite suddenly in 1634 when two dramatists, Jean de Rotrou and Jean Mairet, wrote tragedies in the style of the Ancients in response to the humanist aspirations of their protectors. Now Mairet, through his study of the theory and practice of the Italian dramatists more particularly, had become convinced of the practical value of the codified rules derived by the theorists from the Ancients. In 1634, he set out to apply the rules in a tragedy about the builds his play according to classical principles of progression, using, for example a unified action within a limited time span in such a way as to produce a more powerful effect through concentration than would be possible with a complicated comic imbroglio. An analysis of individual scenes shows within them a masterly concern with form in matters of symmetry and dramatic progression as well as language. While the principle of verisimilitude (*vraisemblance*) may, to our modern minds, be strained by unlikely *dénouements* dictated to a large extent by theatrical tradition, he manages to create central characters in whom there is a judicious balance of caricature and authenticity. And whatever his critics and enemies may have said about verbal ambiguities and his views on religion, there is much more respect for the proprieties in Molière's comedies than in the ancient theatre and the traditional French and Italian farce which were his main sources.[5]

But the greatness of Molière does not, of course, merely depend on his mastery of the rules; it lies rather in his capacity to observe human behaviour with all its frailties, and to use traditions, literary sources, rules and stage techniques acquired over many years of theatrical experience to achieve a rich and critical portrayal of human nature.

This creative tension evident in the comedies of Molière is perhaps more apparent in the field of tragedy, which in many ways epitomizes the classical ideal.

When Pierre Corneille, in 1640, presented the first French tragedy generally recognized as classical, *Horace*, he was already responding to bitter criticism of his earlier work proffered in the name of classical doctrine. At this time, twenty years before Molière produced his first major comedies, tragedy modelled on the works of antiquity had been written and produced in France for nearly ninety years.[6] A significant professional theatre had however been active for only about thirty years of that time. In the early part of the century, alongside humanist tragedies in the Renaissance style, the French theatre had seen some of the excesses of baroque tragedy, a kind of tragedy of blood reminiscent of the Elizabethan stage, often crude in style and construction but characterised by dynamic action. But tragedy had virtually died in France in the 1620s, being supplanted in the theatre by tragi-comedy, and its rebirth had taken place quite suddenly in 1634 when two dramatists, Jean de Rotrou and Jean Mairet, wrote tragedies in the style of the Ancients in response to the humanist aspirations of their protectors. Now Mairet, through his study of the theory and practice of the Italian dramatists more particularly, had become convinced of the practical value of the codified rules derived by the theorists from the Ancients. In 1634, he set out to apply the rules in a tragedy about the

African queen Sophonisba, which he derived in part from the Italian playwright Trissino. In terms of the rules, *La Sophonisbe* is a rather loosely constructed play: the unities of action and place are in fact interpreted rather freely, some elements of the plot would seem more appropriate to tragi-comedy than to tragedy, the situation of the central characters is pathetic rather than dramatic, and the psychology and motivation are sometimes ambiguous and unconvincing. What stands out is the speed with which the action moves, a quality very largely due to the strict application of the unity of time, which is emphasized in the detail of the dialogue. (Sophonisba sees her husband off to battle, learns of his death, meets and marries his conqueror, consummates the marriage and commits suicide to avoid becoming a prisoner of the Romans all in the space of twenty-four hours!) It is clear that Mairet had seen the importance of the idea of concentration which underlies the three unities.

We should not conclude, however, that Mairet was a complete innovator in respect of the application of the unities or the idea of concentration. Insofar as they followed ancient models, usually the plays of Seneca, the dramatists of the sixteenth and early seventeenth centuries had implicitly adopted into the tradition of the theatre some of the principles and techniques later to be proclaimed as rules. If we look at a subject drawn from antiquity for which there was no Senecan model, such as the Coriolanus story, and compare the treatment it receives on the two sides of the Channel, we may have a clearer idea of what is happening in France. You will recall that Shakespeare offers us a kind of fresco retracing all the main events of the life of his hero as presented in Plutarch's *Lives of Famous Men*. The two French playwrights who wrote tragedies on Coriolanus at that time, Pierre Thierry (1600) and Alexandre Hardy (whose play was published in 1625 but written and performed long before this) both limit the action to the latter part of the story, and Hardy, a professional playwright of long experience, begins his drama only at the moment when Coriolanus is accused of treason by the Roman mob and decides to offer his services to the enemy—that is, at the moment when the real tragic conflict begins. We are thus plunged into an already tense situation, which shows Coriolanus as a man of iron will and intense feeling.[7] These dramatists, especially Hardy, thus adopt the principle of beginning the action *in medias res*, as close to the climax as possible, a procedure to be advocated by the theorists of the classical period in order to strengthen the concentration of the drama and make of tragedy essentially a crisis.

In the two and a half years following the production of Mairet's *Sophonisbe*, there appeared two remarkable plays which were to have an immense impact on the development of tragedy in France:

La Mariane by Francois Tristan L'Hermite (performed in 1636) and *Le Cid* by Pierre Corneille (performed in January 1637). (*Le Cid* was originally presented as a tragi-comedy, but in many ways its action is essentially tragic, and some time later, after revision of the text, Corneille styled it a tragedy.)

Both these plays are marked by dynamic action, powerful verse and keen psychological insight. In both cases, the dynamic action is based on a dilemma, a deep conflict which takes place within the soul of the protagonist.[8] King Herod, in *La Mariane*, is torn between his passionate love for his reluctant wife Mariane, whose family he has murdered, and his seething desire to take revenge on her for the infidelity and treason of which he suspects she is guilty. Rodrigue, in *Le Cid*, is torn between the duty to honour and protect the woman he loves and the duty to avenge the honour of his own family by killing his mistress's father. In the first case, the inner struggle is at the level of conflicting passions; in the second, it is at the level of conflicting duties in a society in which honour is the supreme value. In both plays, the pathos is centred initially on the anguish of the dilemma, and in both, the attempt to resolve the dilemma generates dynamic action.

To my mind, this use of the dilemma or inner conflict as a tragic motif is the essential starting-point of classical tragedy, although neither of these plays is yet more than pre-classical. But we must not imagine that Tristan L'Hermite or Pierre Corneille were the inventors of the dilemma as a dramatic device: in tragedy, it first appears in France in a horror play of the baroque theatre (*Rosemonde*, by N. Chrestien des Croix, 1603), and was developed at about the same time with more dramatic skill in an earlier version of the drama of Herod and Mariane by Alexandre Hardy, whose work served as a starting-point for Tristan L'Hermite and was certainly known to Corneille.[9]

In his preface to *La Mariane*, Tristan says nothing explicitly about the rules beyond remarking that he has no intention of filling his work with Italian imitations and studied conceits (which is no doubt a shot at Mairet); his purpose, he declares, is to study the characters of his protagonists. In fact, he observes most of the rules, at any rate as they were interpreted at the time. If we compare his play with that of Hardy, which is clearly his main source, we see that he has concentrated especially on developing the psychological motivation of his characters, which in Hardy's play is rather sketchy. Every significant action is prepared and motivated, and when Herod, wrestling with conflicting passions, tries to resolve his dilemma, which in Hardy's play he does by a rather arbitrary decision, Tristan gives a crucial role to Salomé, the sister of Herod, a sinister character not fully developed by Hardy, who, because of her hatred of Mariane, feeds Herod's anger with suspicion and anxiety to a point where, losing control of himself, he orders Mariane's execution. But once Mariane is dead, Herod's anger and desire for revenge evaporate, leaving only the enduring passion of love, with the result that Herod is plunged into the agonies of remorse and madness. By developing the psychological motivation in this way and at the same time tightening its dramatic structure, Tristan enhances greatly the verisimilitude of the action and raises the play to the level of great drama.

La Mariane achieved enormous success in the theatre and its essential dramatic structure was imitated by others. In various ways, this play marks the definitive orientation of French tragedy towards the dramatic study of character and moral dilemma, which was to reach its highest point a generation later in the tragedy of Racine. Although Tristan seems to brush the rules aside, there is no doubt that, in giving such importance to motivation in character study, he is concerned essentially with the principles of reason, verisimilitude, and the imitation of nature. Tristan's is an early example of the classical tempering of human experience, the apprehension of the universal in the individual.

Pierre Corneille, in composing *Le Cid*, did not set out to conform to the rules of the theorists, but insofar as he did in fact observe them, he seems rather to have been following the tradition of tragicomedy, which was also moving towards a more 'regular' pattern: he manages to pack the action into a period of twenty-four hours, observes the unity of place as it was understood at the time, and achieves a fairly unified action as far as the main characters are concerned; but he does show violence on the stage, introduces a secondary theme which has little effect on the main one, pays little attention to the linking of scenes and often lets verisimilitude be strained. Yet if we compare *Le Cid* with its Spanish source, we see a deliberate movement by the French dramatist towards the unity of action: he simplifies the intrigue by eliminating many secondary episodes and elements of a primarily macabre, religious or spectacular nature, tightens the action and concentrates interest on the moral crisis and the anguish of its resolution. This, more than a preoccupation with minor questions of form, is in the spirit of classicism.

However, Corneille's play touched off a long and bitter literary debate. His critics were mostly theorists, but they included Mairet, who was also a rival dramatist. Richelieu used the quarrel to enhance the authority and prestige of his newly-formed Académie française, which was called upon to arbitrate. The main criticisms made by the theorists were that the basic moral purpose of art was not respected, for the conduct of the protagonists offered a bad example, and the *dénouement* did nothing to punish them for their misdeeds; the rule of the unity of action was undermined by the introduction of a secondary plot, and the action was not true to life, for the subject, although historical, lacked verisimilitude. In spite of these alleged weaknesses, the play had enormous success and still draws packed houses. To the modern reader, especially one more familiar with the traditions of the Elizabethan theatre, such criticisms may seem to have little weight, especially those concerned with the moral lesson. But we have seen that, for many theorists, the didactic purpose of art overrode most other considerations, and the technical requirements, based on the principle of verisimilitude, were devised to give the moral lesson greater force. Corneille was one of the few writers who took the view that the purpose of dramatic poetry is to give pleasure to the spectators, an idea which he claims to derive from Aristotle:

Ainsi ce que j'ai avancé dès l'entrée de ce discours, que la poésie dramatique a pour but le seul plaisir des spectateurs, n'est pas pour l'emporter opiniâtrement sur ceux qui pensent ennoblir l'art, en lui donnant pour objet de profiter aussi bien que de plaire. Cette dispute même serait très inutile, puisqu'il est impossible de plaire selon les règles, qu'il ne s'y rencontre beaucoup d'utilité.[10]

This does not mean, then, that he rejects the idea of moral utility: it is a question of priorities. Nor does it mean that he rejects the rules; for Corneille the rules are only a means to an end:

J'aime à suivre les règles; mais loin de me rendre leur esclave, je les élargis et resserre selon le besoin qu'en a mon sujet, et je romps même sans scrupule celle qui regarde la durée de l'action, quand sa sévérité me semble absolument incompatible avec les beautés des événements que je décris. Savoir les règles, et entendre le secret de les apprivoiser adroitement avec notre théâtre, ce sont deux sciences bien différentes; et peut-être que pour faire maintenant réussir une pièce, ce n'est pas assez d'avoir étudié dans les livres d'Aristote et d'Horace.... Cependant mon avis est celui de Térence: puisque nous faisons des poèmes pour être représentés, notre premier but doit être de plaire à la cour et au peuple, et d'attirer un grand monde à leurs représentations. Il faut, s'il se peut, y ajouter les règles, afin de ne déplaire pas aux savants, et recevoir un applaudissement universel: mais surtout gagnons la voix publique; autrement notre pièce aura beau être régulière: si elle est sifflée au théâtre, les savants n'oseront se declarer en notre faveur, et aimeront mieux dire que nous aurons mal entendu les règles, que de nous donner des louanges quand nous serons décriés par le consentement général de ceux qui ne voient la comédie que pour se divertir.[11]

These last comments were provoked directly by the debate about

Fig. 1   Raphael. The School of Athens. Vatican, Stanza della Signatura,
c. 1510–11.   (Photo: Alinari)

Fig. 2 Bramante. Tempietto. Rome, S. Pietro in Montoria, begun
c. 1505 (?).   (Alinari)

Fig. 3   Bramante. Belvedere, Vatican, designed c. 1505–5. Drawing of work in progress, by G. Dosio (Florence, Uffizi, Gabinetto dei Disegni). (Alinari-Brogi)

Fig. 4 Raphael. Madonna della Sedia. Florence, Pitti. 1514–15—detail. (Alinari)

Fig. 5   Michelangelo. Doni Tondo. Florence, Uffizi, *c.* 1504—detail.
(Alinari)

Fig. 6 Michelangelo. Jonah. Vatican, Sistine Chapel, 1508–12. (Alinari)

VISVS·

Visv Aquila excellit Solis radiantia spectat
Lumina et illæsis fulgura fert oculis

Nos oculo mentis lumen speculemur Olympo
Luce Dei exorta ut diffugiant tenebræ

Fig. 7   Anon Netherlands artist. Sight: The Five Senses. Engraving,
c. 1600

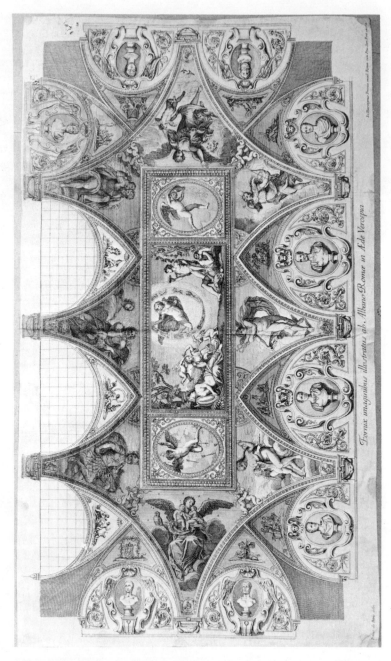

Fig. 8   I. H. Frezza (after Albani). Ceiling (Palazzo Verospi, Rome)
Engraving, 1704

Fig. 9   Claude. Psyche and the Palace of Love. National Gallery,
London (on loan), 1664

Fig. 10   Gaspard Dughet. Tivoli. Hatton Gallery, University of
Newcastle-upon-Tyne. *c.* 1650

Fig. 11   Nicholas Poussin. Landscape with Polyphemus. Hermitage,
Leningrad, 1649

Fig. 12   Claude. Apollo and Muses. National Gallery of Scotland, 1652

Fig. 13   Nicholas Poussin. The Andrians. Louvre, 1627–8

Fig. 14   Gaspard Dughet. Storm: Union of Aeneas and Dido. National
Gallery, London, 1650s

Fig. 15   Nicholas Poussin. Diogenes throwing away his bowl. Louvre,
1648

Fig. 16   Claude. Landscape with Arch of Constantine. Duke of
Westminster Estate, 1651–2

Fig. 17   Medusa Rondanini, (courtesy The Munich Glyptothek, Greek and Roman Sculpture, a brief guide by Dieter Ohly, Verlag C. H. Beck Munchen)

Le Cid. But the fact that Corneille did not reject the rules outright is shown quite clearly in his next tragedy, *Horace*, with which we began this part of our discussion and which many critics see as the first French tragedy which can be considered authentically classical. After *Le Cid*, Corneille, still smarting from the quarrel over the play, produced no new dramatic work for three years and spent much time observing plays and meditating on the dramatic art. The tragedy which emerged in 1640 is carefully constructed according to the rules.

The subject is the story taken from Livy of the inhuman combat fought by three Roman brothers, the Horatii, against three brothers of an Alban family closely related to them by marriage, the Curiatii, to determine whether Rome or Alba would rule in Latium. In the combat, all perish except one of the Horatii, who, when he returns expecting acclaim from Rome, finds himself confronted and challenged by his distraught sister, who had been betrothed to one of the dead Curiatii. In his anger, Horace kills his sister and it is only by special decree of the King in recognition of his great service to Rome that he is exempted from punishment. The action of the play begins just before the point of crisis and moves dynamically through peripateia to its climax at the end of the fourth act, when Horace kills Camille: once we have accepted the basic extraordinary but historical situation, the unity of time serves to tighten the action without any strain on our credibility. We observe the action from one room in the house of Horace, where the protagonists and secondary characters meet and where the news of the battle is reported; the unity of place thus ensures a logical perspective, for the audience has the same limited view of the action as the afflicted families who wait for news, and the tension of the drama is maintained by the fragmentary nature of our knowledge of the events. The action is centred on a confrontation of values which underlies the military confrontation, so ensuring the essential unity of the play, though if we are to believe Corneille himself, because of the 'double peril' to which Horace is subjected (the battle followed by the trial), the unity of action is not complete. And it is precisely this confrontation between patriotic values based on the demands of absolutism and human values based on love and family ties, which gives the play its tragic grandeur. To achieve this result, Corneille has centred his character study on the dilemma between the demands of patriotism and the demands of love which each of the protagonists has to face and has let the major confrontation emerge from the attempts of each one to resolve this inner conflict.[12] This approach goes well beyond the demands of the rules, but the rules provide a sub-structure of unity and concentration without which dramatic force would be lacking.

Here, then, we see tension between the demands of form, as exemplified in the principles and rules of classical theory, and the insight and imagination of a dramatist of genius. But the dramatist does not reject the theory: he interprets it freely according to his practical needs and uses it to discipline and concentrate his material in order to give it greater force.

Corneille undoubtedly had some difficulty at times in coming to terms with the rules, as he himself shows in the examinations of the individual plays published in the later part of his career, where he makes some pungent self-criticism. But in his four most celebrated plays at least, the rules lead him towards careful, disciplined selection of material and the concentration of dramatic elements that we see in *Horace*.

Corneille's younger rival Jean Racine moved significantly further in this direction. At a time when, many years after the composition of *Horace*, Corneille was using more elaborate plots, Racine saw that the essential core of the tragic experience lies in the crisis of inner conflict and the attempt to resolve it. He therefore focused attention on this element and thus moved towards greater simplicity and tightness of structure.

In the first of his major tragedies, *Andromaque* (1667), Racine presents a situation which he seems to have derived from an unsuccessful tragedy of Corneille entitled *Pertharite* (1653)[13]: a chain of unreciprocated love relationships in which a captive is threatened with the death of her child if she does not yield to the advances of her captor and a jealous woman seeks revenge on the lover who has abandoned her. In the Greek setting found for the situation by Racine, Orestes loves Hermione, who however loves Pyrrhus, king of Epirus, to whom she is betrothed; but Pyrrhus loves his Trojan captive Andromache, who however loves only the memory of her dead husband Hector and her child, whose life Pyrrhus threatens. Of this chain of unreciprocated love relationships, which Corneille had not really developed in *Pertharite*, Racine makes a chain of unresolved dilemmas, each dependent for its solution on the outcome of the next and finally on the decision of Andromache. The drama culminates in the dilemma of Hermione, who is torn between her passionate love for the unfaithful Pyrrhus and her intense anger and jealousy at his love for Andromache; when finally Pyrrhus persuades Andromache to marry him, Hermione's anger and jealousy gain the upper hand and she orders Orestes, as the price of her love, to avenge her by murdering Pyrrhus. But when Pyrrhus is dead, her anger, like that of Tristan's Herod, evaporates, and her frustrated love rebounds to plunge her into desperate remorse.

Throughout the play, Racine uses the principles of classical doctrine to concentrate the action and focus it on the study of human character and feeling. In spite of this, he did not escape the attacks of the critics, this time the admirers of the elderly Corneille, who failed to see the power of the drama. It is these critics whom he answers in the first preface to his next tragedy, *Britannicus* (1670), with which they had also found fault:

> Que faudrait-il faire pour contenter des juges si difficiles? La chose serait aisée, pour peu qu'on voulut trahir le bon sens. Il ne faudrait que s'écarter du naturel pour se jeter dans l'extraordinaire. Au lieu d'une action simple, chargée de peu de matière, telle que doit être une action qui se passe en un seul jour, et qui s'avançant par degrés vers sa fin, n'est soutenue que par les intérêts, les sentiments et les passions des personnages, il faudrait remplir cette même action de quantité d'incidents qui ne se pourraient passer qu'en un mois, d'un grand nombre de jeux de théâtre, d'autant plus surprenants qu'ils seraient moins vraisemblables, d'une infinité de déclamations où l'on ferait dire aux acteurs tout le contraire de ce qu'ils devraient dire.

This is clearly a justification based on the classical principles of unity, reason and verisimilitude and the portrayal of human nature.

The extreme point of simplicity in action is reached by Racine in the play he produced at the end of 1670, *Bérénice*. In his preface, Racine sums up the action in two lines of his Latin source, Suetonius:

> *Titus reginam Berenicen, cui etiam nuptias pollicitus ferebatur, statim ab Urbe dimisit invitus invitam.*
> C'est-a-dire que 'Titus, qui aimait passionnément Bérénice, et qui même, à ce qu'on croyait, lui avait promis de l'épouser, la renvoya de Rome, malgré lui et malgré elle, dès les premiers jours de son empire.

The whole play is centred on the dilemma of Titus and the anguish of Bérénice as Titus decides that, for reasons of state, he must not marry the foreign queen whom he loves. Could any action be simpler? Racine justifies his approach in these terms:

> Il n'y a que le vraisemblable qui touche dans la tragédie. Et quelle vraisemblance y a-t-il qu'il arrive en un jour une multitude de choses qui pourraient à peine arriver en plusieurs semaines? Il y en a qui pensent que cette simplicité est une marque de peu d'invention. Ils ne songent pas qu'au contraire toute l'invention consiste à faire quelque chose de rien.

'*Toute l'invention consiste à faire quelque chose de rien.*' Again, an
appeal for verisimilitude through simplicity. A little later in the
same preface, Racine refers to critics who declared that such simple
action could not conform to the rules of the theatre. Having asked
them if they were bored, and learned that, on the contrary, they had
been moved and would gladly see the play again, he asks:

> Que veulent-ils davantage? Je les conjure d'avoir assez bonne
> opinion d'eux-mêmes pour ne pas croire qu'une pièce qui les touche
> et qui leur donne du plaisir puisse être absolument contre les règles.
> La principale règle est de plaire et de toucher. Toutes les autres ne
> sont faites que pour parvenir a cette première.

Here, Racine joins Molière and Corneille in giving overriding
importance to the pleasure of the audience. This is not a rejection of
the rules, of which all three made use in greater or less degree, but
rather an ordering of priorities and an acknowledgement that
principles formulated on the basis of experience and reflection are a
means to an end and not a set of criteria for aesthetic or moral
judgement. And in spite of the rivalry and controversy which
embittered relations between Corneille and Racine, we observe
that, in the field of tragedy, Racine was in fact moving in the same
direction as the young Corneille had done, though with an emphasis
on greater simplicity. For Racine has perceived, as the young
Corneille had done, that true tragedy emerges from the presentation
of moral dilemmas and the anguish of their resolution, which are
given dynamic force by the concentration of elements and the
unification of action imposed by the disciplined classical form.

In the hands of mediocre poets and critics (and they were legion),
the classical rules were commonly a formula for sterility. But the
great dramatists of the age, while often disputing the priority and
interpretation given to the rules by theorists and critics, found in the
principles of classical doctrine a means of disciplining and shaping
their artistic material, thus exploiting the demands of form to
achieve a higher realization of that classical ideal, the portrayal of
human nature. It is through this tension between inherited form and
creative innovation that the classical temper, in their hands, lifts
French drama to the level of great art.

Notes

1. See R. Bray, *La Formation de la doctrine classique en France*, Paris,
    1927 (reprinted Paris, 1951) and H. Peyre, *Qu'est-ce que le
    classicisme?*, Paris, 1965.

2. *La Critique de l'Ecole des Femmes*, sc. VI.

3. 'Premier Placet au Roi sur la comédie de *Tartuffe*'.

4. W. G. Moore, *Molière: a New Criticism*, Oxford, 1949; 1964 edn, p. 103.

5. See, for example, G. P. Shipp, 'A Classicist looks at Molière', AUMLA, xxxix (1973), 51–60.

6. See E. C. Forsyth, *La Tragédie française de Jodelle à Corneille (1553-1640) : le thème de la vengeance*, Paris, 1962.

7. Ibid. pp. 232–5, 338–41.

8. Ibid. pp. 362–70, 389–401.

9. Ibid. pp. 267–82, 341–5.

10. P. Corneille, *Discours de l'utilité et des parties du poème dramatique* (1660).

11. 'La Suivante: épître dédicatoire' (1637).

12. E. C. Forsyth, 'The Tragic Dilemma in *Horace*', *Australian Journal of French Studies*, iv (1967), 162–176.

13. See Racine, *Andromaque*, ed. H. T. Barnwell and R. C. Knight, Geneva, 1977, intro. pp. 7–18.

5
The Classical Temper in Britain:
Origins and Components

Colin J. Horne

A rather Protean concept, as it has already been described in this volume, classicism can be variously defined. Simply, it means the total culture of Ancient Greece and Rome. By transference it implies those same civilized qualities in their recurrent manifestations as identified at various periods and places in history. As an evaluative label it registers a conscious recognition of the preeminence of that past civilization through admiration and the endeavour to imitate and emulate it; sometimes it is elevated to the height of an unattainable ideal. At the level of emulation there is the inevitable implication of adaptation or modification in relation to the peculiar conditions of a later day and age. That is to say that the spirit of an age can be detected as promoting itself in the guise of classicism. The classical temper, so called, is then a mixture of various components, the nature of the mixture changing with the occasion, but normally identified with one or two predominant criteria, such as form, order, reason, balance.

On a wider view, the classical temper represents a recurrent phenomenon in human culture, with its correlative in the individual psyche, representing one pole of an oscillation between restraint and freedom, order and licence, form and diffuseness, authority and freedom, impersonality and individuality, innovation and conservatism. The archetype is something of this kind: freedom runs to excess, excess provokes repression, repression is tempered by rationality to produce compromise and consolidation and stability (which may be taken as classicism); with loss of kinesis stability degenerates into stagnation. And so, usually as the result of some revolution rather than a regular cycle, the whole process begins anew. But it is never precisely the same the next time round and there is usually some kind of progression, or regression, because there is now a more recent past to qualify and transmute the former 'classical' standards. Classicism, that is to say, has not necessarily or entirely produced the new condition of stasis; it is rather a stereotype for identifying and defining the basic, recurrent archetypal elements.

In terms of this thesis classicism in Britain is simply a particular, regional manifestation of a recurrent universal process.[1] If the classics provided a model, they were not necessarily the sole incentive, or even the major cause, of the emergence of the 'classical' temper in Britain. It was part of the *Zeitgeist*, the demand of the age, for reasons of which classical prestige was only one, others being the preceding and resultant political, religious, and economic circumstances; notably the emergence of the revolutionary phenomenon of science, or natural philosophy, as it was then generally called.

The concept of this regional classicism suggests at once the observation that the further from Rome and Athens, from the Mediterranean and the Aegean, the more diluted and transformed, as well as localized, the classical spirit became. In the first place, the direct impact of the culture was qualified by the concurrent mediation through the precedent Italian and French 'classical' modes. Again, there was the matter of climate. Swift, Temple, and others observed that climate affected both the nature of government and the national spirit.[2] It was maintained, not always deprecatingly, that there was something repressive and strengthening in the cold, grey northern climes. To Swift's depiction of the classical spirit as 'Sweetness *and* Light', must be added 'warmth'.[3] And it is just this quality of brightness and warmth, so typical of Mediterranean countries, and so pervasive in the classical aura, that is lacking in the British spirit. Nudity is as incongruous in the British climate, as in its art and literature. For the British, clothing is more significant as symbol and, in its more formal nature as robes and vestments, signifies rank, office, trade, class, etc. Likewise their poets are more intimate with Cynthia than with Apollo. The nude statue looks so blanched and frigid in the British climate, and classical architecture in the cold, grey granite of Scotland is likewise a grim anomaly.[4]

There is another preliminary consideration to be ventilated. If classicism is to be regarded in its most obvious connotation as emulation of classical culture, the question at once arises as to what particular era or area of that culture is to be regarded as most representative and central, and therefore to be taken as the model. The history of Greece and of Rome covers a considerable time span and embraces, as does its art, architecture, literature, philosophy, and political organization, a considerable range of achievements. Neither in fact nor concept can the ancient world be considered a simple or a single unitary phenomenon.

Similarly with the manifestation of classicism in the modern world: how is it to be defined and delineated in any meaningful way? If we regard it simply as direct or mediated access to ancient culture, with admiration and emulation, not always to the point of acceptance of its absolute authority, then in Britain classicism can be identified in some measure or form from the Renaissance at the end of the fifteenth century through to the Victorian period. Though the Renaissance began with the recovery of Greek learning, by and large the British have manifested a closer affinity with Rome and its Empire. Sensitive to the achievements of the ancient world, it was nevertheless in no single way, but many, that England, or Britain, responded to its culture, its forms, its achievements, and took them as some kind of model. Even so, this particular variety of classicism was quite as much the expression of a distinctly national and historical process, and this process it was assisted to identify and direct by an awareness of classical precedents. Nevertheless the classical mode was, I opine, never as dominant or authoritative in England as it was in Italy and France. Always there was what I may term 'the impurity' of British classicism, that is, the truly indigenous nature of the adaptations it effected.

Those features in the history of English culture that can be denominated as classical were, in large measure, the products of, firstly, the Civil War in the seventeenth century and its resolution; of Protestantism; of emergent Capitalism, its mercantilism and the rise of the bourgeoisie; and, above all, of science or natural philosophy. Classicism provided both a reinforcement and a sanction for the ideals and necessities arising from these historical movements, just as they themselves often assumed the accoutrements and vesture of classicism to sustain them and clothe them with authority. This contention can be illustrated by a brief and highly selective survey of some of the respectful adaptations of the classics in English literature of the sixteenth and seventeenth centuries. They do not so much subserve ancient models as exploit them for the promotion of an emergent national culture.

Writing as he did with truly classical precision and poise, Sir Philip Sidney may be regarded as the earliest exemplar of the classicist as, appropriately, aristocrat, soldier, and hero. As a puritan, it can be argued, he was no less classical in his serene didacticism on moral issues. Astutely he drew on Aristotle, Plutarch, and the Renaissance humanists Scaliger and Minturno to refute the Platonic censure of poetry. It may be, as Saintsbury long since observed, that it was 'the defence, not so much of Poetry as of Romance'.[5] Certainly Sidney was one of the first to challenge the domination of the doctrine of 'truth to nature' in its restricted Aristotelian sense. He contended that the poet can improve on Nature:

lifted up with the vigor of his own invention, [the Poet] doth grow in effect into an other nature: in making things either better than nature bringeth foorth, or quite a new, forms such as never were in nature.[6]

The erotic poetry of that other brief-lived early blossom of the Elizabethan age, Christopher Marlowe, is resonant with echoes of Ovid and springs from the rich soil of classical mythology. The exuberant product is nonetheless quite unclassical in its voluptuous description and its sensational hyperbole, such as the vision of Helen:

> Was this face that Launcht a thousand ships,
> And burnt the toplesse Towers of *Ilium*?
> *Doctor Faustus*, ll. 1768-9)[7]

English is a literature, especially in the period of the Renaissance, distinguished by its achievement in drama, yet that drama was shaped surprisingly little by classical precepts or models. How unfruitful the potential connection was can be seen in such negligible early plays as *Jocasta* and *Gorboduc*, both in the Senecan strain, and both of them aberrations from the mainstream of English drama. Almost nothing was derived directly from the greater drama of Greece. Shakespeare, with his 'little Latin and lesse Greek', achieved his apotheosis with a blithe unawareness, or disregard at least, of the hitherto supreme drama, which he was to equal, or even overtop, on a twin but separate peak. Even when he turned to ancient history for his material, such as the careers of Julius Caesar, Antony and Cleopatra, or Timon of Athens, it was mediated by more or less contemporary translators and freely ⁱᵃⁱnted, with little concern for historical accuracy, classical codes ⁱⁱour, or Aristotelian precepts for drama.

ⁱⁱc drama of Dryden was moulded more by French ⁱᵃⁱal originals. There was of course Ben Jonson, ⁱⁱed classical scholar. His plays, in the ⁱᵃracters in English, have a classic social context, together with ⁱtion, that, presented with clarity ⁱnuinely classic achievement. In right, physical vigour, however, his and heartily English, in both their istics.

classical literature, the epic, the only English ⁱ ⁱessfully for the Parnassian height was, of course, Mⁱⁱ ⁱ of its subject and in imaginative range, *Paradise Lost* has ⁱ ⁱly no rival, even in antiquity. Milton supremely exemplifies the adaptation of classicism in England to serve the contemporary needs of religion, and of a highly moral Puritan ethic in particular. Towards the classics Milton's attitude remained richly ambivalent. It was Milton who described Rome, though putting the words into Satan's mouth, as 'great and glorious Rome, Queen of the Earth'. This superb vision of classical grandeur, to which Milton himself is obviously committed, is used by Satan in a vain attempt to lure Christ to damnation. Significantly for the age in which Milton wrote, Satan is enabled to make the glory of Rome visible by the aid of the new inventions of science:

> strange Parallax or Optic skill
Of vision, multiplyed through air, or glass
Of Telescope,

and focused in detail by Satan's 'Aerie Microscope'.

(Paradise Regained, IV. 40–3, 57)

It was this new science, of course, that was ultimately to outclass the power and the authority of classicism.

What we have here is, admittedly, a view of Rome in its decline. More compelling is the next vision:

> *Athens* the eye of Greece, Mother of Arts
And Eloquence, native to famous wits
Or hospitable, in her sweet recess,
City or Suburban, studious walks and shades,   (IV. 240–3)

and so on, at great and splendid length. The passage is perhaps the most resplendent poetic conspectus of the components of Greek civilization ever written, a noble panegyric. Christ rejects it outright in a succinct and knowledgeable review of the whole course of Greek philosophy as 'false, or little else but dreams, / Conjectures, fancies, built on nothing firm', at least when compared with 'Light from above, from the Fountain of Light' (ll. 292–3, 289). He gives the pre-eminence to the Hebrews. Matthew Arnold summed it up memorably, 'Milton was born a humanist, but the Puritan temperament mastered him.'[8]

In this conspectus of classicism the crucial period for the classical temper in Britain is the period 1660–1785, or more focally, the four or five decades spanning the turn of the century in 1700. The 'classical temper' of the age was, in its components and aspirations, peculiarly British in manner and, more than ever, shaped by the pressures of the time. Classicism, thus adapted, was the prestigious stereotype for just what the age needed in the way of consolidation after a remarkably vigorous but divisive period in the political and religious life of the country. Culturally at least, the new temper represents a confluence of currents, not all of them classical in origin, but all of them flowing to a resolution in intellectual, moral, and political tenets that are appropriately and traditionally termed classical.

With Richard Bentley in the forefront, it was undeniably a great age of classical scholarship in Britain. More pervasively, the unity and cohesion the country needed were recognizably available in the bond of a classical education among the educated and ruling classes. Never before or since was there so much adoption, imitation, and application of the matter and method, the rules and precepts, of classical literature, art, and architecture.

In the literature this is everywhere apparent in the prevalence of classical allusions, the concern with the rules of writing derived mainly from Aristotle and Horace, and the resort to classical models, as well as innumerable translations, most various in their degree of faithfulness to the originals. As Dryden's Crites observed of the Ancients, 'we do not onely build upon their foundations; but by their modells.'[9]

In practice this was not simply a matter of slavishly copying classical authors. For English literature, like the culture more generally, the classics were valuable for their practical utility in providing an almost hallowed exemplum of control and restraint, as much as for their innate virtues generally. As Professor Hardy has remarked in the introduction to this volume, 'The ancient world has stood as a cultural ideal; yet in other ways, too, it has been used as a means of authorizing or justifying particular innovations or points of view.'[10]

From Oldham and Dryden, through Pope, to Johnson, one of the most fruitful developments was the so-called 'imitation' of a classical poem, usually a Latin satire of Juvenal or Horace. The process was one of rewriting the original in contemporary terms. The impact of the piece was partly determined by the reader's recognition of its consonance with the original, while yet counter-pointed by a departure from some of its basic features, even a reversal of them. Such, notably, is the character of Orgilio in Johnson's poem *London*. While professedly imitating Juvenal's third satire, Johnson blends the Verres and Persicus of the original to produce what was probably intended to be a satirical portrait of Sir Robert Walpole.[11] More striking still is the moving conclusion to *The Vanity of Human Wishes*, written in imitation of Juvenal's tenth satire. Undeniably Christian in spirit, there is nevertheless implicit in it a touchingly personal confession of inability to accept that faith with unquestioning conviction.[12]

My concern is with this kind of practice, the application of the classical mode to a later and different age and nation as an apposite support and justification of contemporary endeavours. It is a commonplace that by the end of the seventeenth century Britain transparently needed a period of consolidation, marked by moderation, and promoted by reason, balance, good sense, all of them traditionally regarded as traits of classicism, though by no means consistently exhibited in the actual history and culture of Greece and Rome.

With Roman history in particular the parallel seemed to be pertinent. By a little convenient adjustment, the course of Roman history through kings, republic, and emperors served in its general lines as a prototype for the progression of English history from Henry VIII, through the Civil War and Protectorate, to the rule of the Stuarts and Hanoverians. As we shall see, writers were especially sensitive to the potential projection implicit in the decline and fall of the Roman Empire. Though this period we are presently concerned with is now commonly known as the Augustan Age, one must not forget that Pope and others, while promoting the Emperor Augustus in Virgilian terms as a pattern of the patron of the arts, were not unmindful of his other role as despot. Thus Thomson emphasizes that, when 'the first smooth CAESARS arts caress'd, / Merit, and virtue', they were only 'simulating' liberty (*Liberty*, III. 484–5). There was an important distinction. Britons saw themselves as living in an age politically superior to that of the Roman Augustans; after the Revolution of 1688 their kings were constitutional monarchs, subject to the overriding constraints of British liberty and democracy. As we shall see, it was a conviction of the new nationalism that the political principles, supposedly emanating from Greece and Rome, had found their apotheosis only in 'BRITAIN's matchless Constitution' (*Liberty*, IV. 814).

Such classical analogues, often more specious than this, were prevalent in the literature. When Whig supporters of Marlborough adduced parallels from ancient history for the supposed ingratitude of the nation to its victorious general, Swift countered by drawing up a pair of balance sheets as an ingenious demonstration that Marlborough had received from the nation six hundred times as much, in equivalent monetary values, as any victorious Roman general. That was in No. 17 of *The Examiner* (16–23 Nov. 1710). In the very next number Swift again employed the classics and the current respect for them to denounce Lord Wharton in the style of Cicero orating against Verres. Early in his career he had similarly manufactured from classical history a camouflaged projectile for discharge in the contemporary political war. His *Discourse of the Contests and Dissentions between the Nobles and the Commons in Athens and Rome* (1701) was launched in defence of the Whig Junta against their impeachment by the Tories. The parade of ancient historical events is a palpable disguise; the ideas behind them, as well as the purpose, are demonstrably contemporary and mainly those of Sir William Temple.[13]

Horace was incontestably one of the most admired of classical poets at this time; his writings were basic to the culture of the age, constantly quoted, translated, and imitated. Here again there was frequently an ulterior motive. The Horatian doctrine of the virtue and ease of the retired rural life, of the Sabine farm, set against the greed and luxury of Rome, was suggestively promulgated for socio-political ends. It comforted and supported the landed interest in its resistance to the pressure of the moneyed men and the new mercantile power of London.

The composite and tendentious nature of the classical temper in Britain at this period is nowhere better exemplified than in the poetry of the anglicized Scotsman James Thomson. Solid rather than subtle as poetry, it is nevertheless the most instructive attempt at a synthesis of the new culture, with its components of historicism, Protestant morality, the new philosophy of science, the ascendant British world trade and the accompanying imperialism. All are viewed in the light of ancient history and classical values. They are presented in a quasi-classical style in poems of a novel kind, ingenious blends of elements of pastoral, georgic, and epic. Thomson promulgates the new patriotism and its emergent nationalistic aspirations as the culmination of the classical tradition. At the same time he identifies it with the optimistic philosophy of progressivism. Though the values of classicism were a stabilizing force in the period, they were not, as commonly supposed, restrictively conservative. On the contrary, classicism provided a firm base for a leap into modernism.

'Lo the resistless Theme, Imperial *Rome*.' So proclaims John Dyer in the opening of the descriptive, meditative poem *The Ruins of Rome* (1740), supposedly written *in loco*. So it was for Thomson, and for others before and after them. Britannia, in Thomson's poem of that title (1729), is

A State, alone, where *Liberty* should live,
In these late Times, this Evening of Mankind,
When *Athens*, *Rome*, and *Carthage* are no more,
The World almost in slavish Sloth dissolv'd.　　(ll. 200–3)

The general import is that Britain will regenerate the world and make itself pre-eminent by taking over from 'the most high and palmy state' of Roman imperialism and Greek democracy. 'Liberty' is the theme, as it is of his longer poem with this starkly monumental title. It is enshrined in 'BRITAIN's matchless Constitution'

(IV. 814) and upheld by the Protestant ethic of stern morality and freedom of conscience. The courage and success of Rome's 'resistless legions' (III. 93) are adduced as a particular object for admiration by Britons. But Britain has other and better means to promote the cause of universal freedom. As 'mistress of the main', Thomson prophesies, speaking in the role of Liberty herself, the British navy will dominate the world as Rome's legions did, and bring universal peace. And the means? Not conquest but commerce:

> Round social earth to circle fair exchange,
> And bind the nations in a golden chain.   (IV. 437–8)

And the ultimate vision? That will be realized when

> commerce round the world
> Has winged unnumbered sails and from each land
> Materials heaped that, well employed, with Rome
> Might vie our grandeur, and with Greece our art!   (V. 570–3)

Thomson in fact is aligning trade with the purpose currently asserted for the new science, 'the universal benefit of mankind'. This is the altruism of capitalism, and for Thomson there is nothing paradoxical about it. Just that same combination of idealism and practical utility, in the moral sphere, was attributed to a classical education.

Furthermore, to the precepts of classical philosophy could be added the admonitory example of ancient history. Gibbon was not the first to be fascinated by the decline and fall of Rome. As Francis West notes further on in this volume, though the 'classical temper ... did not exclude the idea of human progress ... how this had happened interested writers less than how such a civilized classical or neoclassical world might decline and fall'.[14] Contemplating that 'vast monument, once-glorious *Rome*' (*Liberty*, I. 18), Thomson, like Dyer and Gibbon later, sounds the note of hubris. Britain, in its glory the inheritor of Roman grandeur, could ultimately suffer the same 'miserable fate / Of an heroic race' (I. 322–3). Rome fell when 'tame Corruption taught the servile herd / To rank obedient to a master's voice' (I. 80–1).[15] Dyer elaborates the warning about the new prosperity of the new capitalism in his vision of a once mighty nation 'Dissolv'd in Ease and soft Delights', and all the 'Brood of voluptuousness', 'Bane of elated Life, of affluent States' (*Ruins of Rome*, ll. 470, 490, 536). To this Thomson adds 'Another species of tyrannic rule' that destroyed Rome, the temporal power and 'idiot SUPERSTITION' of the Roman Christian church (*Liberty*, IV. 49, 76).

It is another reminder that classicism in Britain was always tempered by the awareness that the Ancients were pagan. Britain was emphatically a Christian country and, for good and ill, pugnaciously Protestant at that. Good and ill, for to this also there was a dual aspect. The solid moral preoccupation of Protestantism readily related to the classical concern with the whole duty of man as a moral being. On the other hand, the irrational, disruptive extreme of the radical Dissenters was deprecated as 'enthusiasm', and Swift was not alone in castigating and curbing the aberration by an application of the rational, moderating spirit of classicism. It is in fact reasonable to detect a marked congruence between Protestantism and classicism in the temper of Britain, one respect in which, especially in the insistence on liberty of conscience, it differed from the monarchical and authoritarian spirit of the classical temper in France.

The other powerful shaping force at work in Britain, only emergent then but destined in time to be arguably more dominant than either Christianity or classicism, was of course the new natural philosophy, modern science. At just this time, the last decades of the seventeenth century, in the notable if not notorious altercation known to history as the Ancients versus Moderns controversy, the new science and ancient civilization were set up as rival contenders for the intellectual crown, with religion looking on as an uneasy third party. The obvious claim for the superiority of the Moderns, of course, lay in the new epistemology and the future potential of science, that is, as specified by its proponent, William Wotton, '*Natural History, Physiology,* and *Mathematics,* with all their Dependencies'.[16]

On this view science was the source, as it was certainly the dynamic, for the new conception of progressivism, the conviction, not just the hope, that civilization is a continuous linear process of improvement. As against this, the assertion that the Ancients had already achieved the finest products of the mind and could never be equalled, let alone surpassed, could only be viewed as at best conservative but more obviously regressive. The main contention of this paper, however, is that the role of classicism was often regarded in Britain as conducive to the political, moral, and cultural advancement of the country. On that view, I think, science and classicism can be seen in retrospect as allied in the prevailing temper of that time that still goes under the name of classical rather than scientific.

The degree to which they were in step was less apparent to contemporaries. At the very time, for example, that the natural philosophers were rejecting Aristotelianism, the authority of Aristotle in literary criticism was being revived and exalted. In an intermediate position, as Kearney has put it, 'The Scientific Revolution, though it originated in the recovery of Greek science, led to the overthrow of the Greek way of interpreting the universe.'[17] In other respects strong support for the optimistic, progressivist view of history could be drawn from the classics. As Basil Willey has explained, 'Greek wisdom presupposed that human nature was perfectible, or capable of indefinite improvement through moral training.'[18] The most reasonable conclusion to the issues raised in this dispute was that the Ancients had laid the foundations, set some of the essential standards and, pertinent to all occasions, could continue to stimulate and sustain the advance of mind.

Classicism and science, therefore, were at least compatible in unifying the British people and inspiring them with a new and confident sense of their destiny, cultural, political, and imperial. Ancients and Moderns were consonant in their insistence on rationality, objectivity, and universal order, the prevalence of law in nature and society. The basic inductive method of science and the spirit in which it was applied to the dispassionate observation of the natural world had the aim of seeing life clearly and seeing the total scheme of things. In the early days of the Royal Society its apologist Thomas Sprat proclaimed that science is directed to 'the practical ends of Life:—[it] opens our eyes to perceive all the realities of things', its goal, to lay the foundation of 'a Philosophy of *Mankind*'.[19]

The most fundamental principle of classicism was, I suppose, 'to follow Nature', that is, to discover and emulate the universal order of things in all its rationality and harmony. To follow nature, at the end of the seventeenth century, could only mean to move forward into vast new realms of knowledge. Dryden's Crites again speaks for the new age: 'Is it not evident, in these last hundred years—that almost a new Nature has been revealed to us?'[20] By 'nature', the classical thinkers had meant mainly human nature. In a recognizably similar spirit the new science was extending that concern to the material world. One product was 'nature poetry', springing up all along the road to Wordsworth. Also, with respect to the doctrine of the wisdom and goodness of Nature, and reverting to an earlier contention in this paper, one notes that commerce again fitted readily into the well ordered complex of the classical temper. 'Providence has adapted nature to trade,' wrote Defoe, 'and made it subservient in all its parts to the several necessary operations of commerce.'[21]

In conclusion, I am going to suggest that the representative figure for the classical temper in Britain was not one of the great men of antiquity, Plato, Aristotle, Homer, Virgil, or Horace, neither Julius Caesar nor Augustus, but a contemporary national hero, Sir Isaac

Newton. The new composite spirit of the age is apotheosized in this genius of the new science. For eighteenth-century England Newton became a folk hero of epic stature. As such his name is recurrent in the literature. In illustration I turn again to Thomson, this time to his *Poem Sacred to the Memory of Sir Isaac Newton* (1727). It was Newton who, 'The Heavens ... To their first great Simplicity restor'd', revealing creation,

> The finished university of things
> In all its order, magnitude and parts.

Grand simplicity, unity, universality, all these are the criteria of classicism. At the same time, and pre-eminently, Newton's motivation as presented in the poem was the truly Christian one,

> to adore that Power
> Who fills, sustains, and actuates the whole.
> (ll. 82–4, 140–1, 142–3)

Over all the ancient nature gods Newton had supremely elevated the Christian deity as essentially the God of Nature.

The tribute begins and ends, significantly for my further contention about the regional and patriotic spirit of the British classical temper, by enthroning Newton himself as both universal genius and national hero:

> And what the Triumphs of old GREECE and ROME,
> By his diminish'd, but the Pride of Boys
> In some small Fray victorious! when instead
> Of shattered parcels of this earth usurp'd
> By violence unmanly, and sore deeds
> Of cruelty and blood, Nature herself
> Stood all subdued by him, and open laid
> Her every latent glory to his view. (ll. 31–8)

By a paradoxical reversal of the classical precept to follow Nature, Nature is finally to be conquered (or is it seduced?) and controlled, through science, for the universal benefit of mankind and the peace of nations.

This fine ideal in which the classical temper culminated was strangely awry in its forgetfulness of the classical insistence on plain reason and commonsense. That same noble illusion, arising pre-eminently from the direct link between a classical education and colonial administration throughout the nineteenth century, was to inform and inflate the spirit of British imperialism in its rise to power immeasurably greater than Rome's. Some stale, sad odour of it still haunts that nation in its decline.

Notes

1. I am deliberately using the term Britain in recognition of the contribution, sometimes quite distinctive, of Scotland and of England's colonies in Ireland and America. Of that contribution there is no space for separate mention here.

2. Cf. Sir William Temple, 'Of Poetry', *Five Miscellaneous Essays by Sir William Temple*, ed. S. H. Monk, Ann Arbor, 1963, pp. 199–201; Jonathan Swift, *The Sentiments of a Church of England Man, Works*, ed. H. Davis, Oxford, 1939, ii. 17. It was a belief widely diffused, especially among Deists.

3. Swift, 'The Battle of the Books', in *A Tale of a Tub, . . .*, ed. A. C. Guthkelch and D. Nichol Smith, Oxford, 1958 (2nd edn), p. 235.

4. In this context it may be remarked that not the least significant element in the dilemma of Australian culture has been the strain of trying to reconcile a tradition of north-western European culture to a habitat that, in the more populated part, the south of Australia, more closely resembles the Mediterranean area. The Australian abroad always tends to shuttle between Britain and the southern European countries, experiencing an affinity with each.

5. G. Saintsbury, *A History of English Criticism*, Edinburgh and London, 1949, p. 54.

6. *The Defence of Poesie, . . .*, ed. A. Feuillerat, Cambridge, 1912, 1962, p. 8

7. *The Complete Works of Christopher Marlowe*, ed. Fredson Bowers, Cambridge, 1981 (2nd edn), ii. 220.

8. 'Equality', *Mixed Essays*, London, 1879, p. 80.

9. *An Essay of Dramatick Poesie, The Works of John Dryden*, vol. xvii, ed. S. H. Monk, Berkeley–Los Angeles–London, 1971, p. 15.

10. See ante, p. 2.

11. Cf. J. P. Hardy, *'London'*, in *Reinterpretations: Essays on Poems by Milton, Pope and Johnson*, London, 1971, pp. 113–20.

12. Cf. J. P. Hardy, 'Hope and Fear in Johnson', *Essays in Criticism*, xxvi (1976), 296–9; C.J. Horne, 'The Opening of *The Vanity of Human Wishes:* Johnson's Observation and the Elevated Manner', *AUMLA, Journal of the Australasian Universities Language and Literature Association*, xlix (1978), 19–20; J. P. Hardy, 'Johnson's *Vanity of Human Wishes*', *Studies in the Eighteenth Century IV*, ed. R. F. Brissenden and J. C. Eade, Canberra, 1979, pp. 93–8.

13. Cf. the introduction to the edition by F. H. Ellis, Oxford, 1967, pp. 161–2.

14. See post, p. 110.

15. Thomson's more immediate political purpose, to asperse the peace

policy and the 'corruption' of Walpole's administration, was recognized from the beginning. In this respect *Liberty* was a cogent contribution, on the grand scale, to 'dissident Whig panegyric'. See Cecil A. Moore, 'Whig Panegyric Verse, 1700–1760: a Phase of Sentimentalism', *Publications of the Modern Language Association*, xli (1926), 362–401.

Though this bias in the poem is not my present concern, it serves not at all to diminish but rather to emphasize the authority and contemporary appeal of this 'classical' conception of British history and Britain's destiny that Thomson was reinforcing. His intention, certainly, was to write a poem more noble and dignified than would suffice for the exigencies of political journalism. As Johnson observed, 'Upon this great poem, two years were spent, and the author congratulated himself upon it as his noblest work' (*Lives of the English Poets*, ed. G.B. Hill, Oxford, 1905, iii. 289).

For the definitive study of these matters, see further, A. D. McKillop, *The Background of Thomson's 'Liberty'*, The Rice Institute Pamphlet, xxxviii (1951), no. 2.

16. W. Wotton, *Reflections upon Ancient and Modern Learning*, London, 1705 (3rd edn), p. 18.

17. H. Kearney, *Science and Change 1500–1700*, London, 1971, p. 9.

18. *The English Moralists*, London, 1964, p. 30.

19. *The History of the Royal Society of London, For the Improving of Natural Knowledge*, London, 1667, pp. 26, 63.

20. See n. 9.

21. *Review*, vol. i, no. 54 (3 Feb. 1713).

6

Characteristic Traits of Viennese Classicism

Georg Feder

The word 'classical' does not seem to have been used with musical connotations before the seventeenth century,[1] though similar words had been used in the sixteenth and early seventeenth centuries by authors of Latin, Italian, and German treatises on music when they were recommending as models the works of a growing number of composers of the latter part of the fifteenth or of the sixteenth centuries. Heinrich Schütz, a great composer himself, in the preface to his *Geistliche Chormusik*, a collection of his motets published in 1648, called such composers 'classicos autores'.

In the second half of the eighteenth and in the early nineteenth century, compositions as well as composers were sometimes called classical. This seems to indicate that individual works had come to the fore. The term has also been applied to styles. Vocal polyphony of the sixteenth century and especially Palestrina's compositions have been called classical because the purely vocal or *a cappella* style was brought to perfection in that century and in that composer's works.

The term has also been applied to the period of Haydn, Mozart, and Beethoven. Some critics recognized only Haydn and especially Mozart as classical composers while others included Bach and Handel.[2] The different meanings of the word 'classical' hardly lend themselves to its unspecified use. Therefore musicologists in our century prefer the term 'Viennese Classicism' when they speak of the later works of Haydn and Mozart and the earlier ones of Beethoven.

The general style of this period of music history has also been referred to as classical, but most writers hesitate to call the individual compositions by Boccherini, Pleyel, Cherubini or their minor contemporaries classical. Even in its musicological use, the word has maintained some of its connotations of quality, which prevents us from completely reducing it to a purely technical term.

The word 'classical' does not seem to have been applied to the music of Antiquity, though Antiquity was a model in some respects also for musicians. Writers on music during the Renaissance used to mention the miraculous effects ascribed to music in ancient Greece. Ancient theory of rhythm as well as classical rhetoric influenced musical terminology and composition for many centuries. The Florentine Camerata and the circle around Jacopo Corsi sought to revive the musical style of Greek drama, which was monodic rather than polyphonic, and in the process invented opera. But they knew even less of Greek music than we do now.

Much knowledge about musical life in Antiquity has been assembled from literary sources and iconography in recent years. But our knowledge of the music itself is small. Though the Greeks knew a kind of notation, only the verse has been transmitted through the centuries in written form; the music has not, except for a few fragments. Greek music theory was recorded and has been better preserved. It was a basis for a rational music theory in the medieval liberal arts and later on, but is rather ambiguous as far as its more practical implications are concerned.

Musical notation was indispensable for the rise of Western European music. So was polyphony. When in the ninth century the monks of several European monasteries began to write down in rather vague neumes a repertory of Gregorian chant, its melodies had probably been in practical use for a while. Notation was descriptive rather than prescriptive. But with the development of artificial polyphonic composition in the thirteenth century and with the growing independence and integration of simultaneously sung vocal parts, notation gradually shifted towards rationalization and was used by composers in a prescriptive way.

Polyphonic music not only grew more artificial, it also broadened its emotional scope. The tradition of Western art-music was originally purely vocal and sacred. Composers opened the path for a more comprehensive musical expression of man's emotions with the setting into music not only of sacred, but also of secular texts. Later, they began to use musical instruments, which ecclesiastical authorities had earlier condemned as works of the devil.[3] They also wrote compositions for a dominating solo vocal or instrumental performer, that is, compositions which allowed music to express more individual emotions. Nevertheless, the instrumental as well as combined vocal and instrumental styles never wholly abandoned the basis of the vocal style. In classical instrumental music, the instruments, as it were, sing.

Sociological factors were important, too. Plain-chant had been by anonymous composers. Composers of polyphonic music became known by their names. Their works began to show individual features. But composers usually remembered that they had a specific function in society. They were thinking of the performers and the listeners of their music.

There apparently had not been many listeners when polyphony originated. Polyphonic music had started in small ecclesiastical circles and won the interest of wider circles gradually. With the rise of opera in the seventeenth and eighteenth centuries, music became an increasingly important part of cultural life in centres like Venice, Naples, London, Paris, and Vienna. The public included connoisseurs and amateurs.

The Classical composers considered the tastes of both. Popularly flavoured tunes or rhythms are essential ingredients of Viennese Classicism. Neither Haydn nor Mozart, not even Beethoven, except perhaps in his last string quartets, disregarded the tastes of the public, in spite of the fact that they improved rather than totally accepted them. The agreement between a leading composer and his public has perhaps never been greater than in Vienna around 1800. The enthusiasm aroused by the performances of Haydn's oratorio *The Creation* in 1798 and subsequent years united members of the high and low nobility and of the middle class. The work's immediate success in almost all parts of Europe was unprecedented in music history.[4]

This work and many others by Haydn, Mozart, and Beethoven became part of the traditional musical repertory and have stayed in it. The same is true of some works by Corelli, Handel and a few other composers. Some of Bach's works have also been transmitted uninterruptedly from his time to ours, while others have fallen into oblivion, like most music composed in the preceding centuries, not only works of minor value, but also works once highly appreciated. These have been studied by musicologists in the nineteenth and twentieth centuries or revived by the endeavours of historically minded editors, publishers, and practical musicians.

The works which had never been forgotten and quite a few of those which experienced a kind of 'Renaissance' have stayed in the repertory long enough to be rightly judged. Nevertheless, no musical composition has existed long enough to be compared with the works of classical literature and art. This may give rise to some doubts about the reason for calling any musical composition classical and for using this epithet when there is scarcely any connection with Antiquity to be seen. But this may be an overly restrictive point of view. Certainly there has been an admirable progress in polyphonic music, leading to compositions that can compare with the works of such arts as boast a longer tradition.

The driving force behind the rise of European polyphonic vocal and instrumental, sacred and secular, ensemble and solo music was the continuous interplay of two contrasting principles. These have been called tradition and innovation, collectivism and individualism, order and freedom, or something else. Music theory was mainly guided by the first of these principles. It formulated and thereby stabilized the basic rules by which composers had worked. The sum of these rules was an internationally accepted tonal grammar of European musical language. It changed little by little during the centuries, perhaps faster than linguistic grammar did, but it was sufficiently conservative to support the continuity of polyphonic music and ensure the comprehensibility of new compositions.

Equally important was a traditional musical vocabulary. Composers used compositional elements that could be remembered and recognized. Typical motives, sequences, cadential formulas, schemes of modulation, rhythmic patterns, and ways of word-painting were such elements. Composers more or less varied them and combined them into varying superstructures. These, as well as the musical vocabulary, had a close affinity to the musical genre to which a composition belonged. The system of genres was also traditional and changed slowly. Together with other fairly constant factors, all this contributed to a mutual understanding of composers, performers, and the educated public.

On the other hand, all three parties were increasingly interested in novelty. When the old musical vocabulary had been used many times and had become obsolete, it could not convey aesthetically meaningful messages any more. It then descended from the higher level of expression to the lower level of musical material. Such material could possibly be reshaped or built into new super-structures to convey new messages. A well known cliché like a cadential formula could take on new meanings. Haydn, for example, used the seemingly insignificant cadential formula of a sequence of dominant and tonic chords ending the first section in the final movement of his 'Farewell' symphony and built it into a rather long period in the development section (Symphony No. 45, Finale, measures 53–6 and 80–97).

Individuality was highly rated at the time of Viennese Classicism. Immanuel Kant defined genius as the talent or natural gift which gives art its rules.[5] Nevertheless, tradition continued to play an important part. The Classical composers never abandoned tradition, even though they more or less transformed it. Beethoven did so more intensively than Haydn and Mozart had done. When the process of innovation accelerated in the nineteenth and twentieth centuries, the balance was lost and the common understanding of composers, performers, and the public decreased.

It is, however, difficult to discover a single spiritual force lying behind the music of the last decades of the eighteenth century and the first one or two of the nineteenth. Viennese Classicism was influenced by diverse trends in the spiritual climate of its age. Haydn's and Mozart's mass compositions reflect the splendour of baroque Austrian churches, Haydn's *Creation* reflects the optimism and rationalism of the Enlightenment, Mozart's *Magic Flute* the humane ideas of Freemasonry, Beethoven's *Fidelio* some of the ideas of the French Revolution, his Third Symphony the heroic spirit of the era of Bonaparte, his Ninth the idealism of Schiller. Traces of classicism in the sense of an imitation or emulation of Antiquity can be seen in the librettos of Mozart's serious operas *Idomeneo* and *La clemenza di Tito*; the first libretto was based on a French Tragédie lyrique of the year 1712, the second followed a Metastasian libretto of 1734. The librettos of Mozart's comic operas follow the tradition of Italian Opera Buffa, which harks back to the tradition of Italian Commedia.dell'arte.

Viennese Classicism hardly reflects Winckelmann's ideas of 'noble simplicity and sedate grandeur'. If we search for composers who better agreed with this ideal, we may find them in Gluck and some mid-century composers of vocal music like Johann Adolph Hasse[6] or Carl Heinrich Graun, whose principles of composition were perfect in their own way but rather simple when compared with those of their predecessors Johann Sebastian Bach and Handel or of their successors Haydn and Mozart. 'Noble simplicity' or 'simplicity and dignity' were the catchwords of the rationalistic simplifiers of German Protestant church-music of that time.[7] Haydn sometimes gave the directions 'semplice' and 'innocente-mente' in his scores, but these words should not be mistaken for a description of his style as simple and innocent.

Viennese classicism did not make music simpler. It made it simpler only through the reduction of the Rococo element. Otherwise it made it instead more complicated, not for the sake of complication, but in order eventually to be more interesting and diversified in its emotional content than it had been in the mid-century. Haydn and Mozart achieved a similar complexity to Handel and Bach in the first half of the century, but they did so by principles of composition different from those of Handel and Bach.

One of these differences was a dynamic concept of musical form, strange as this may seem when one thinks of classicism in terms of order and restraint. It was the baroque era that had preferred thematic and motivic unity, melodic continuity, equilibrium of rhythmic flow and consistency of texture. This perhaps indicates that it is problematic to transfer the concepts of the history of art to the history of music. Anyway, Pergolesi in his comic intermezzo *La serva padrona* (1733) was perhaps one of the first composers to try discontinuity of melody and rhythm.[8] The Classical composers adopted his innovation and developed it.[9] Haydn varied, split, and differently combined the motivic material of a movement and rather freely distributed it among the instrumental parts.

A more dynamic concept of form was also achieved by the application of contrast at different levels of a composition. Mozart favoured the contrast of two motives supporting each other in one theme. A similar kind of dualism was often used by Beethoven, who contrasted a more energetic first theme with a gentler secondary theme, each balancing the other in one movement. Nevertheless, the musical process was coherent. Haydn now and then liked to surprise the players and listeners of his music with sudden, though well-prepared silence. It is the seemingly paradoxical function of these interruptions to raise the tension of the music's progress and thereby strengthen its coherence.

Baroque music and especially arias had owed much of their coherence to the repetition of an unchanged ritornello. Haydn in the arias of his Italian oratorio *Il ritorno di Tobia* of the year 1775 still followed this practice. In his *Creation*, however, the instrumental introduction, the interludes and the postlude of an aria vary according to the moods expressed.[10] A similar freedom is found in the overall form of arias. The *Da capo* aria, still prevailing in the earlier oratorio, was given up by Haydn in the later work in favour of less predictable forms. The aria *Rollend in schäumenden Wellen* ('Rolling in foaming billows') begins like a typical D Minor aria depicting the restlessness of the sea. Haydn previously had written several arias of this type in his cantatas and operas.[11] This time he does not follow the type throughout but continues with images of the mountains, the plains, and the river, and ends with an idyllic musical picture of the words 'im stillen Tal der helle Bach' ('in a quiet dale the clear brook'). The music depicts a changing scenery; it ends in a mood very different from that of the beginning. There is no *Da Capo* or ritornello restoring the initial mood as would have been normal in preclassical times.

Haydn did not achieve this kind of freedom in all of his works. A comparison of the final chorus in his *Orlando paladino*[12] and the vaudeville which concludes Mozart's *Die Entführung aus dem Serail*[13] shows the difference between a more conventional and a more dramatic form. Mozart's German *Singspiel* was performed in Vienna in July 1782, Haydn's Italian *Dramma eroicomico* in Eszterháza in Hungary in December that year. In Mozart's opera, each of the five characters sings a stanza which is followed by a refrain sung by all of them together. In Haydn's Finale, the singers alternate in a similarly regular way and also unite after every stanza.

When Rodomonte, the bellicose king of Barbary, sings his stanza in Haydn's finale, the minor mode is used, and a shade falls upon the lovely music, more for the sake of variety than for dramatic reasons. The following Tutti and the next stanza, sung by Alcina, are also in the minor mode even though the words would not demand it. Through this procedure Haydn achieves a mildly contrasting middle section, after which the major mode returns. The homogeneity of the piece is never really disturbed; unity is attained rather automatically by use of a symmetrical form.

In Mozart's vaudeville, Osmin does not remain in harmony with the four characters who have sung before him. When it is his turn, he starts the melody in a way similar to that in which the other persons had, but then can't control his feelings any longer. He deviates from the gentle song and bursts out with a repetition of part of his fierce aria: 'Erst geköpft, dann gehangen, dann gespießt auf heißen Stangen' ('first beheaded, then hung,' etc.). The other persons are so greatly embarrassed that they do not continue the melody required by the form of a vaudeville but sing a different melody appropriate to the situation. Only then they find their way back to the refrain. The surprising brightness and blitheness of the immediately following chorus of the janizaries concludes the opera. In the combination of the vaudeville and the concluding chorus, unity is achieved not so much through a regular muscial form (as in Haydn's chorus) as by an underlying emotional process.

Another result of a freer approach to composition was the combination of different styles and techniques as structural elements in one work. Mozart's great operas *The Marriage of Figaro, Don Giovanni*, and *The Magic Flute* combine serious and comic elements and thereby reflect human life more truly than pure Opera Seria or pure Opera Buffa could have. Haydn in his late oratorios achieved a similar synthesis by combining the praise of God with a loving description of the earth and of man.

North German critics, accustomed to the more uniform style of the Baroque and of the mid-century, disapproved of Haydn's juxtaposition of 'learned' and popular styles, of serious and comic elements, and of the introduction of the minuet into the symphony. As late as around 1800, some of Haydn's contemporaries were concerned about the stylistic diversity of some of his works. Friedrich Schiller, who liked the more uniform style of Gluck's operas better, denounced Haydn's *Creation* as a 'charakterloser Mischmasch'.[14] As late as in 1826, the Swiss composer Hans Georg Nägeli criticized the juxtaposition of *cantabile* style and passage-work in Mozart's instrumental music as 'widerwärtige Styllosigkeit'[15] (disagreeable lack of style).

The Classical composers' eclectic choice of heterogeneous

material mostly passes unnoticed nowadays because we have become accustomed to it. We notice only the most obvious instances
like the Turkish music in the *Entführung aus dem Serail*, or the
strange song of the Men in Armour in Mozart's *Magic Flute* written
in the style of a German Protestant chorale prelude, or the
unaccompanied military trumpet signal in the music of the dungeon
scene of Beethoven's *Fidelio* and his *Leonore* overture, or the
psalmody-like *a cappella* intonations preceding each one of the
Seven Last Words of Our Saviour in Haydn's oratorio of that title.
All these examples show the well calculated use of a different idiom
for a special function in a new context.

A more subtle mixture of styles was achieved by the integration of
contrapuntal devices into compositions which were otherwise
dominated by melody. Haydn, after some experiments in his earlier
years, used counterpoint in his symphonies and string quartets not
as an end in itself, as was the case in the Baroque era, but rather as a
means to achieve a diversified whole. The same motivic material is
sometimes presented first in a version dominated by popular
melody and then in an artful contrapuntal version, as in the final
movement of Haydn's symphony no. 101 (Finale, measures 1–28
and 190–250).[16] Mozart combined the main motives in the Finale of
his *Jupiter* symphony[17] in a contrapuntal development of even
greater complexity.

The synthesis of styles resulted in diversity and more complex
structures. It also resulted in a greater assimilation of different
genres. Haydn, Mozart, and, to a lesser degree, Beethoven, followed
tradition when they used more or less different styles for different
genres, places, and even persons. But at the same time they worked
towards a more universal style, towards an equal weighting of all
genres, of all works in a genre, of all movements in a composition
and of all sections in a movement.[18] The norm they implicitly
followed was that of the symphony. An anonymous author in a
Leipzig music periodical deplored in 1806 that the symphony as it
was created by Haydn and Mozart was then exerting its power over
other genres like the concerto and the piano sonata and that operas
were symphonies with song.[19] The spread of the four-movement
form from the symphony to the piano trio and the piano sonata,
where it had not been customary, is clearly seen in Beethoven's Op.
1 and 2. However, Beethoven did not adhere to this form. He also
used different forms. An all-embracing uniformity was avoided.

There is no way of defining any musical style except in comparison with others. I have described some of the elements and
circumstances of Viennese Classicism in the light of the history of
European polyphonic music. I have also described some of its more
specific traits as opposed to those of the earlier part of the eighteenth

century. My description would have been different had I taken the point of view of the nineteenth century. The elements of order and discipline would have overshadowed those of freedom and imagination in the works of Haydn and Mozart. Haydn would have mainly appeared as a forerunner of Mozart and Beethoven. Beethoven would have appeared even more distant from Haydn and Mozart than he has in my paper. Mendelssohn's relation to Classicism would have needed discussion. The oft-discussed relation of Classicism and Romanticism would have come into play. Some music critics in the years around 1800 called romantic what we call classical. Later in the century Romanticism was seen as opposed to Classicism. Friedrich Nietzsche thought there was no classicism in music at all but only Counter-Renaissance, Baroque, Romanticism, and *décadence*.[20]

I have stressed the innovative features in the music of Haydn and Mozart. We should, however, remember that the Classical composers did not search for novelty for its own sake. Mozart more than Haydn, and Haydn more than Beethoven, obeyed limits of expression. They did so partly for reasons of tradition, partly for purely aesthetic ones. Polyphonic music had for centuries been considered an aural pleasure. While the music of Haydn, Mozart and Beethoven was far more than that, it continued to be 'harmonikal' as well as harmonious, especially Mozart's music. For him, more than for Haydn and Beethoven, beauty predominated over expression, although he also well knew how to express *terribilità*[21]—we need only to think of his *Don Giovanni*. The incomparable balance of content and form in Mozart's music was best described by Mozart himself in a letter of 26th September, 1781. He was then composing his opera *Die Entführung aus dem Serail*. In this letter he stated that 'passions, strong or not, must never be expressed to a disgusting extent and that music even in the most dreadful situation must never offend the ear but should always be pleasant and consequently should always be music'.[22]

Notes

1. Ludwig Finscher, 'Zum Begriff der Klassik in der Musik', *Bericht über den Internationalen Musikwissenschaftlichen Kongreß Leipzig 1966* (Cassel–Leipzig, 1970), 109.

2. Arno Forchert, '"Klassisch" und "Romantisch" in der Musikliteratur des frühen 19. Jahrhunderts', *Die Musikforschung*, xxxi (1978), 422 ff.

3. Reinhold Hammerstein, *Die Musik der Engel*, Berne–Munich, 1962, p. 114.

4. Friedrich Blume, *Syntagma musicologicum*, i (Cassel, 1963), 555.

5. *Kritik der Urteilskraft*, sect. 46.

6. 'Classical qualities' have been observed by Sven Hansell in Hasse's vocal works; *The New Grove Dictionary of Music and Musicians*, viii (London, 1980), 287.

7. F. Blume *et al.*, *Protestant Church Music, a History*, New York, 1974, p. 324.

8. Thrasybulos Georgiades, 'Aus der Musiksprache des Mozart–Theaters', *Mozart Jahrbuch*, i (1950), 78 ff.

9. Georgiades, 'Zur Musiksprache der Wiener Klassiker', ibid. ii (1951), 50 ff.

10. Anke Riedel-Martiny, 'Das Verhältnis von Text und Musik in Haydns Oratorien', *Haydn-Studien, Veröffentlichungen des Joseph Haydn-Instituts, Köln*, i (Munich, 1967), 221 ff.

11. 'Quanti il mar tesori aduna' (from a cantata, 1763?), 'Varca il mar' (from *Le pescatrici*, 1769), 'Mille lampi' (from *Orlando paladino*, 1782).

12. Joseph Haydn: *Werke, herausgegeben vom Joseph Haydn-Institut, Köln, Reihe XXV, Band 11* (2 vols), ed. Karl Geiringer, (Munich, 1972–3), Kritischer Bericht, 1973.

13. Wolfgang Amadeus Mozart: *Neue Ausgabe sämtlicher Werke, Serie II, Werkgruppe 5, Band 12*, ed. Gerhard Croll, Cassel, 1982.

14. Letter to Ch. G. Körner, 5 Jan 1801.

15. Hans Georg Nägeli, *Vorlesungen über Musik mit Berücksichtigung der Dilettanten*, Stuttgart and Tübingen, 1826, pp. 157 ff.

16. Haydn: *Werke, I/17*, ed. Horst Walter, 1966; Kritischer Bericht, 1972.

17. Mozart: *Neue Ausgabe sämtlicher Werke*, IV/11/9, ed. H. C. Robbins Landon, 1957; Kritischer Bericht, 1963.

18. As far as the movements in a composition are concerned, cf. William S. Newman, *The Sonata in the Classical Era*, Chapel Hill, N. C., 1963, p. 143.

19. *Allgemeine Musikalische Zeitung*, viii. 616 ff.

20. *Der Wille zur Macht*, sect. 842.

21. Cf. John Gregory's paper, ante, pp. 18 ff.

22. '. . . weil aber die Leidenschaften, heftig oder nicht, niemal bis zum Ekel ausgedrücket sein müssen, und die Musik auch in der schaudervollsten Lage, das Ohr niemalen beleidigen, sondern doch dabei vergnügen muß, folglich allzeit Musik bleiben muß . . .'; Mozart: *Briefe und Aufzeichnungen, Gesamtausgabe*, ed. Wilhelm A. Bauer and Otto Erich Deutsch, iii (Cassel, 1963), 162.

7
Weimar Classicism as a Response to History

Anthony Stephens

This essay is based on the postulate that the aesthetics of Weimar Classicism show analogies to the tensions evident in its creators' understanding of contemporary history and, more specifically, that such tensions are indicative of a more general crisis in the German Enlightenment's reaction to the French Revolution. Before attempting to define Weimar Classicism or to describe its historical context, I would like to take Goethe's commentaries on two works of classical antiquity as points of orientation in order to show one fundamental achievement of classical art as he saw it. When Goethe was living in Rome in December 1786 he mentions in a letter the Medusa Rondanini (Fig. 17), a Roman copy of the early Imperial age of a Greek original from the end of the fifth century B.C. What fascinates Goethe from the outset is the paradox expressed by this sculpture: on the one hand its formal beauty, on the other what he calls 'the fearful stare of death'.[1] Two years later he described it as 'a strange work that, as it expresses the dichotomy between death and life, between pain and the delight of the senses exerts ... an inexpressible charm upon us'.[2] Almost forty years after Goethe first saw the Medusa, he received in 1825 a cast of it as a gift of King Ludwig of Bavaria and in his letter of thanks he once again evokes the dualism of the work: 'the head of Medusa, horrifying in legend by virtue of its baneful effects, appears to me in this form as beneficent, as having healing powers.'[3] At about the same time he writes to a friend, that this Medusa does not petrify but rather 'splendidly animates the artistic sense'.[4] For Goethe, as for many of his contemporaries, the triumph of classical art was frequently seen as *directly* reflecting a wholeness and harmony of experience. But in his comments on the Medusa Rondanini he goes beyond the conventional response and sees the miracle of classical art in its power of transformation: to take that which is in itself terrible or horrifying and to transmute it through artistic form into something which heals rather than destroys, and this, paradoxically, without diminishing the reality evoked. The head of Medusa still conveys for Goethe what our minds cannot assimilate in its raw state, 'the fearful stare of death', but the power of art translates this into beauty, which for Goethe always has life-giving powers. Another work of sculpture which fascinated Goethe over many years and on which he wrote abundantly is the Laocoön, a work which had caused much controversy in eighteenth-century Germany and which had served for Lessing as an occasion to define the separate areas of achievement proper to literature on the one hand and the visual and plastic arts on the other.

Goethe's own essay on the Laocoön was written in 1797, in his most 'classical' phase, and is strongly influenced by his reading of Aristotle's poetics. He says the figure of the younger son evokes in us pity, the figure of the elder son fear, whilst the figure of the father produces 'Schrecken', a sudden, violent emotion whose meaning in English lies somewhere between fright and terror. But, as in the case of the Medusa Rondanini, Goethe sees the whole power of art in its ability to transmute, to transform the negatives of suffering and death into what he calls 'a spiritual and sensuous totality'. From this sculpture he explicitly draws a moral for all art: the artist triumphs not only by infusing quiet and simple objects with his aesthetic sense, but also and equally when he succeeds in moderating and containing through artistic form the passionate outbursts of human nature.[5] Thus Goethe agrees with Winckelmann that the first and obvious achievement of classical art is to create an aura of 'noble simplicity and quiet grandeur', but he reserves his highest praise and greatest sympathy for that art which assimilates the unassimil-able, that translates terror into beauty, that confronts the most chaotic elements in human feeling and action and moderates them, but in doing so does not diminish or dilute their primal reality. In this sense classical art triumphs by the harmonious resolution of paradoxes and in these formulations Goethe sets an implicit standard for his own artistic endeavour which he was usually not to reach, particularly when the challenge of the unassimilable did not derive from a mythical past, but from contemporary history.

None the less, the inclusion of the destructive, the terrible within the serenity of a self-consciously 'classical' work is certainly part of Goethe's intentions when writing *Iphigenie auf Tauris*, a distant relation of Euripides' drama, which Goethe finished in 1787 and which is usually held to mark the beginning of Weimar Classicism. Goethe's *Iphigenie* is a play that is very hard to love and harder to stage effectively. Even Schiller, in the years of his closest collaboration with Goethe, found the play too sententious and rarified for it to generate any warmth. Of the figure of Iphigenie herself he says: 'She is moral and nothing other than moral; but the sensuous force, the life, the movement and everything else that makes a work genuinely dramatic—all this she lacks.'[6] What Goethe had done was to sacrifice the whole supernatural apparatus of the Greek original to the cause of making his play one long debate on ethics. Action is kept to a minimum, both the gods and the furies are reduced to aspects of the human psyche and such ideals of conduct as the play offers are puzzling and, in the case of the heroine, seem to amount to maintaining one's purity through determined non-involvement. While writing the play, Goethe was impressed by what he called the 'healthy, self-assured virginity' of Raphael's St. Agatha and he resolved to let his heroine 'say nothing which this saint herself could not have said'.[7] And yet, behind all this stylized serenity there lurked, for Goethe himself, the forces of chaos and rebellion. Looking back on writing the play, Goethe concedes in his autobiography: 'also the more desperate members of that line, Tantalus, Ixion, Sisyphus, were at that time my saints . . . antiquity had already seen their fates as truly tragic, and if I succeeded in showing them as the members of a monstrous opposition in the background of my *Iphigenie*, then I am indeed indebted to them for part of the effect which this play was fortunate enough to produce.'[8] From this it appears that in Goethe's own concept of the drama the enforced tranquillity of the surface is meant to become transparent, to permit a glimpse of a 'monstrous opposition' in the background, the whole violent story of the race of Tantalus, so that Iphigenie's own rejection of involvement, her apparent incapacity for passion, might be seen as a conscious reversal of the history of her house. I do not think the play succeeds fully in doing this, but in Goethe's intentions, at least, we may perceive the same principles at work as are present in his commentaries on the Medusa and the Laocoön. Art reaches its highest achievement when it contains the chaotic, but still leaves it visible, even if as a threatening presence in the background of a scene in which the gods have been replaced by ethical principles.

The label 'Weimar Classicism' has something monolithic about it, as if it could be confidently applied to a whole age of German culture, to a well codified school of aesthetic doctrine with clearly defined aims and prohibitions. And there was indeed a time when all of this appeared to be true, but it was not the time when Goethe and Schiller were actually writing and it is no longer in the present day. The monumentality of Weimar Classicism was largely a myth created in the middle of the nineteenth century and sustained within Germany until the late sixties, when it came under a critical scrutiny from which it has not recovered. In the middle of the nineteenth century, not only the greatness of some of their literary achievements, but also the rising tide of German nationalism, created a situation in which a classical epoch was desirable for reasons of national pride. The process of myth-making was begun two years after Goethe's death by a scholar named Gervinus who claimed: 'Goethe and Schiller led the way to an ideal of art of which no one since the Ancient Greeks had had more than the vaguest inkling.'⁹ There is here an implicit slur on the Italian, English, and French versions of classicism and also the implicit denial of Goethe's and Schiller's own debts to these other traditions. German classicism is seen as deriving from the pure Greek source alone, and the fact that Goethe, for example, took the trouble to translate Voltaire's drama *Mahomet* and that Schiller felt this act significant enough to warrant writing Goethe a long poem about it, in which he manages to say that French classical drama, for all its rules, was still less than morally pernicious—facts like these tend to go unmentioned in the nineteenth century's monumentalizing of Weimar Classicism. In 1905 an influential scholar Bernhard Suphan, holding a festival oration at the twentieth gathering of the Goethe Society in Weimar, intoned: 'And so the Two stand there for us like splendid trees who have interwoven their crowns and their roots. Like two high eucalyptus trees they have been planted in the declivities of our being, to ward off the noxious vapours of the depths, to rid the land of fevers and to breathe health upon it.'¹⁰

Following a common pattern of mythicizations, the German myth of Weimar Classicism had the effect of increasing the prestige of its origins and exaggerating its legacy. If one looks at the reality, what is most striking is the hesitant, modest and experimental character of Weimar Classicism as Goethe and Schiller created it. Goethe's *Iphigenie* is often cited as the classical work *par excellence*, embodying perfectly Goethe's ideal of Humanity, but it is a work which Goethe conceived in considerable uncertainty and continued for many years to have grave doubts about, as Schiller records.¹¹ It was originally written in prose, this version was rejected, and there followed a considerable struggle to get it into iambics, so that far from being the embodiment of a finished theory or being written according to the formal principles of an established school, the 'classical' quality of this play was quite literally something which Goethe created by trial and error and about which he continued to have second thoughts for at least a decade afterwards. As against the myth, there is in the reality of Weimar Classicism always the quality of improvisation, and a glance at any complete works of Goethe immediately shows how many improvisations did not come off, like the drama *Nausikaa* or the epic poem *Achilleis*. Another hindrance to gaining access to the reality stems from the German

way of looking at German literature as opposed to a broadly
European perspective. German has two words, 'Klassik' and
'Klassizismus' corresponding to different meanings of the English
'classicism'. 'Klassizismus' means roughly the imitation in art of
models from antiquity, the assigning to certain aspects of antiquity
an exemplary meaning for modern life and the adherence to certain
norms allegedly derived from antiquity, even if the derivation is
often suspect. 'Klassizismus' is thus a phenomenon that can occur
in all artistic traditions without necessarily dominating the scene.
The term can be used pejoratively for a slavish and sterile imitation
of ancient models, and Goethe himself did just this in an essay on
contemporary Italian painters. German literature in the latter half
of the eighteenth century and at the beginning of the nineteenth was
riddled with manifold forms of 'Klassizismus', practised by writers
who had little or nothing to do with Weimar Classicism.[12] 'Klassik'
on the other hand has wholly positive connotations in normal
German usage, is appplied commonly and inaccurately to the whole
epoch in which Goethe and Schiller were creative, and is defined in
German encyclopaedias as relating to 'original creations of
exemplary value and of the highest ethical and aesthetic rank'.[13]
Whilst Goethe and Schiller themselves were usually quite diffident
in the claims they made for their work, a nationalist posterity, ever
intent on making them seem *more* than just writers, has often
exaggerated the exemplary, ethical dimension—witness Suphan's
view of Weimar Classicism as a kind of cosmic disinfectant.

Another problem in assessing the reality of Weimar Classicism is
caused by the divergence of the German view from the European
view. For Weimar Classicism is embedded in the wider context of
European Romanticism, and it is really only in German scholarship
that it is seen as standing quite apart from Romanticism. To other
eyes, it blends. If we take a venerable and emphatically non-
German treatise such as Jacques Barzun's *Classic, Romantic and
Modern*, then we find Goethe treated throughout as a Romantic,
and allowed to be 'not a Romantic' on only three occasions.[14] Now,
to traditional German literary history at least, this is a heresy. The
very fact that Weimar Classicism is contemporaneous with the
Romantic movement in Germany has impelled German scholarship into minimizing commonalities and over-stressing differences
to the point where the European perspective may be lost altogether.
Goethe himself helped by saying at one point that Classical was
healthy and Romantic was sick.[15] Unfortunately, what was no more
than a casual piece of literary polemics has incited some German
scholars to treat it as if it were a passage of scripture, and much
confusion has resulted. Despite the fact that professed German
Romantics were as enthusiastic about their vision of Classical

Greece as were Goethe and Schiller about theirs, or that a poet such as Hölderlin, who emphatically does not belong to Weimar Classicism, was far more dependent on an ideal of Classical Greece for his entire artistic creation than ever Goethe and Schiller were, the legend of the fundamental incompatibility of Classicism and Romanticism in German literature at the turn of the nineteenth century enjoyed well over a hundred years of vigorous life.

With the questioning of the whole concept of Weimar Classicism in Germany there has been some dismantling of the barriers built against Romanticism and it has become recognized that there are many Romantic influences on the late Goethe. Over the last decade, the prime question for German scholarship has tended to be: is there anything worth saving of the concept of Weimar Classicism?

There may well be if one applies the more modest concept of a 'classical temper' in the sense of the effective combination in the creative process of elements which are also integral to either the Enlightenment or to Romanticism but which are there placed in the service of different syntheses. The concept of a classical temper also allows us to do justice to the personal quality of Weimar Classicism. Unlike French Classicism, which is metropolitan in its flavour and aristocratic in its assumptions, reflecting the elaborate codes and tensions of a sophisticated court society, Weimar Classicism is provincial in its origins and constantly striving away from them into more august, imaginary realms, becoming in the process more private in its terms of reference. Whilst located at the small court of Weimar, it draws little moral sustenance from the institution itself and rather reflects the quandary of middle-class emancipation in a context where dependence on the aristocratic world is no longer ethical or intellectual but has become no more than institutional. There is, therefore, sense in continuing to talk about Weimar Classicism, if one restricts it to the works and aspirations of Goethe and Schiller between about 1786 and Schiller's death in 1805 and recognizes that there is much in Goethe's work after the end of the collaboration that remains faithful to the ideals on which he and Schiller were agreed. Certainly both Goethe and Schiller had an awareness of the lack of a classical epoch in German literary history, and certainly both tried to remedy this lack by a didactic initiative, launching periodicals to promote a certain style in literature and the fine arts and polemicizing against trends which they found inimical to the development of a classical and national literature in their own sense. But another element left out of the myth of Weimar Classicism is the lack of resonance of their efforts outside Weimar, which was very much a small town in Germany. The eight-volume edition of Goethe's works in 1790, offering the public for the first time such works as *Iphigenie, Tasso, Egmont,* and a substantial fragment of *Faust,* ramained largely unsold and did not attract any pirate editions. The list of subscribers contained no more than 303 names.[16] The periodicals Goethe and Schiller launched were short-lived and were far from fulfilling their purpose. Young writers did not become disciples, and both Weimar Olympians made some appalling misjudgements of the most talented of the younger generation.

Hence, to preserve the reality of Weimar Classicism a certain amount of scaling down is necessary. But it is only a scaling down of the myth, and the myth itself is a product of the *later* transformations of German nationalism. For nationalism, as Goethe and Schiller knew it, was the quite laudable process by which German writers in the eighteenth century strove to overcome Germany's cultural cringe towards France and establish a unified German culture in despite of the political disunity which saw German-speaking peoples divided among more than three hundred political entities. The nationalism that developed around the middle of the nineteenth century and had its first culmination in the Franco-Prussian war of 1870–1871 has little in common with nationalism as Goethe and Schiller understood it, although they were posthumously pressed into its service and monumentalized in the process of German self-exaggeration that marks the Wilhelmenian period. Schiller's poem to Goethe on his translation of Voltaire's play is an interesting document of the emergence from cultural inferiority that is closely synonymous with Goethe's and Schiller's concept of a national literature. The poem begins with a mock-heroic reproach to Goethe for having anything to do with French literature at all: 'You yourself, who led us away from false obedience to rules back to Truth and Nature, you, a hero already in your cradle, who strangled the serpent that was constricting our genius ... you are now found sacrificing on the ruined altars of a false Muse'—and the word Schiller uses for a 'false Muse', 'Aftermuse', is more than derogatory.[17] Schiller now sees, or pretends to see, this liberty endangered by the mere fact that Goethe has translated a play.

It is important to see the beginnings of Weimar Classicism as part of such a process of emancipation. As they understood it, classicism was not something that Goethe and Schiller were ever confident of achieving by even their best efforts and one reason for this lack of confidence was that they saw their own efforts in a pronouncedly historical perspective. The creators of Weimar Classicism were acutely, indeed sometimes oppressively, aware of the nexus between historical conditions and the production of literature. This may be shown by exploring some of the contradictions and tensions in both authors' view of the French Revolution.

In 1795 Goethe published in *Die Horen*, a periodical edited by Schiller, an important essay called *Literarischer Sansculottismus*. The title promises a response to literary radicalism, with a sideswipe at one of the manifestations of the Revolution Goethe liked least, namely the participation of the lowest classes in it. The essay is polemical, an attack on someone who had lamented in print the lack of truly classical authors on the German literary scene. Goethe does not claim that there *are* authors of classical stature in Germany — rather, he denies it and then lists the conditions under which classical literature in his sense may arise. Classical authors may flourish, he says, when in a nation's history great events and their consequences form a happy and meaningful unity; when greatness is evident in the thoughts of the people, depth in their feelings, and strength and logic in their actions; when the authors themselves, imbued with the national spirit, are able by virtue of their innate talent to feel sympathy with both past and present; when the nation has already such a high degree of culture that their own education offers them no hindrances ... then one may expect classical literature in the most positive sense. Goethe then goes on to point out that none of these conditions are fulfilled in the German speaking world of his time. He laments the lack of any centre around which German culture can form itself. And the blame falls not upon the German authors themselves, who are doing their best in adverse circumstances. Nor does it fall on the Dukes, the Princes, the feudal system, the problems of middle-class emancipation, but on something rather amorphous: on the Century, on History.

> Every man, even the greatest genius, suffers from his own Century in some respects, just as he profits from it in others ... But one should not make it a reproach to the German nation, that its geographical situation holds it tightly together, whilst its political condition breaks it into a thousand pieces. Let us not wish upon it the upheavals which could prepare the way for classical works in Germany.[18]

We can see from this something of the dilemma in which Goethe and Schiller found themselves at the time of their collaboration, namely 1794 till 1805. Were they charged with trying to create classicism in Germany, both would have had to plead guilty — but this despite all their best insights into the historical situation of their own culture and the determination of literature by external circumstances. There is a bitter irony about the last sentence quoted above: it contains the recognition that a national literature equal to Goethe's own ambitions could only arise in a different political order from the present one, but it rejects revolutionary change as a way of achieving that order. It is the kind of attitude that Marx was later to attack, saying that the Germans were merely 'philosophical contemporaries without being historical contemporaries', which he amplified in his introduction to Hegel's philosophy by saying, 'The Germans have *thought* in politics what other peoples have done . . . they have partaken in the development of modern nations only through abstract thought, without actively and effectively taking sides in the real struggles essential to this development'.[19] Here Marx was following in the footsteps of Heinrich Heine who had already made similar observations.

Goethe's statement is also interesting in the light of the fact that the autonomy of the work of art was one of the doctrines dearest to Weimar Classicism and one of its main legacies to German literature since, and yet in the essay of 1797, he insists on the nexus between literature and history to the point where his own efforts would seem to be doomed to failure. The extreme tensions here may remind us of the tensions within his concept of the highest achievement of classical art with which I began: classical art in its highest form turns terror into beauty, assimilates the unassimilable; classical literature in Germany cannot be produced in the given historical situation, but yet for that very reason it will be attempted, as a contradiction to history and without recourse to revolutionary change. The two sets of tensions stand in an analogical relation to one another; it remains to be seen whether the connection is more than an analogy. Goethe and Schiller did not invent the doctrine of the autonomy of art for Germany—that honour would seem to go to a theorist named Baumgarten in 1750—but they certainly made it one of the programmatic goals of Weimar Classicism, although Goethe, for one, does not seem to have entirely believed it was attainable. But this is consistent with the image of Weimar Classicism as nothing monolithic, but rather an experimental process, set moving in response to an historical dilemma to which there was no clear solution, with self-imposed criteria that might well be impossible to meet and with full awareness of the riskiness of the undertaking.

It is well known that many German writers initially greeted the French Revolution with enthusiasm and that most turned away in horror from the events of 1792–93. Goethe was opposed to the Revolution from the outset and Schiller played a waiting game until he too was disgusted by the course events had taken with the execution of the King and the mounting number of victims of the Terror. But, whatever the emotional reactions may have been, the Revolution posed an intellectual problem to those who had proudly felt themselves to be part of the European Enlightenment, and this Goethe and Schiller both did after they had outgrown their early phase of youthful revolt.

We can see the nature of the problem better if we look at a work by an obscure writer called Adam Bergk, published in 1795 and posing in its title the question: *Does the Enlightenment Cause Revolutions?* Bergk's answer is an unqualified 'yes' and he goes on to say that this is something that partisans of the Enlightenment should be proud of:

> By altering and expanding man's intellectual horizons, by making man aware of those demands he ought rightly to make of society, writers of the Enlightenment necessarily pave the way for revolutions, and they bring them about if there is no relief of the pressure that builds up when citizens declare a state of affairs unjust because it conflicts with their human rights. What reason is there then for acquitting writers of the honourable charge that they contribute to revolutions? To do so would be to distort the truth and abandon its service as cowards. Would it not mean saying to these writers: take off your human nature like a suit of clothes and become—Heaven knows what! Any such nonsense would be an insult to Reason, contempt of Mankind and could only find favour with cowards, egocentrics or immature minds.[20]

Compared with the endless paradoxes produced by Goethe and Schiller in trying to come to terms with the Revolution, there is a refreshing simplicity about Bergk's position, but only because he is apparently able to accept the inhumane and sensational consequences of the Revolution as a necessary part of the Enlightenment's continuation. To do so at the time was no mean feat, particularly as it became clearer in the course of the Revolutionary Wars that the new France was bent on the complete economic exploitation of those German states it occupied. Weimar did not suffer this fate, securing ten years of neutrality in the treaty of Basel in 1795, but Goethe's and Schiller's abhorrence of post-Revolutionary France was none the less for that. In a letter to Herder of the same year, Schiller says:

> Therefore I know of no other salvation for the Spirit of Poetry but that it should withdraw from the region of the real world and instead of entering upon any coalition ... should direct all its energies towards total separation. Thus it seems to me a great triumph for the poet that he creates his own world and, through the agency of the Greek myths, remains the kinsman of a distant, foreign and ideal age, since reality could do nothing but befoul him.[21]

Accordingly, Schiller's works in his classical phase avoid contemporary settings, are concerned with history mainly as a treasury of moral examples and largely shy away from finding analogies to the French Revolution in either the historical or legendary past. His drama *Wilhelm Tell* does explore social conflict and class antagonism leading to concerted action, but the theme of revolution in the sense pertinent to the late eighteenth century is kept at bay. Schiller's Swiss represent a healthy and intact society in harmony with Natural Law which successfully beats off a threat from outside itself. While the watchword may be 'Liberty', fruitful parallels to the French Revolution are virtually absent. Schiller's most important contribution to the debate on Enlightenment and Revolution comes in his letters 'On the Aesthetic Education of Mankind', to which I shall return. Schiller was anything but reticent about his determination *not* to come to terms with his age. In a programmatic essay announcing his periodical *Die Horen* in 1794 Schiller writes: 'But as the limited concerns of the present increasingly excite, constrict and subjugate men's hearts, all the more urgent the need becomes to liberate them once more through a general and higher concern with that which is *purely human* and elevated above any influence the times may have, and in this way to unite the politically divided world under the banner of Truth and Beauty.'[22] Schiller writes as if the turning away from the sordid realities of history to the realm of pure aesthetics was a *fait accompli*, executed with great conviction and some panache. But another acute observer of the time, the Romantic Friedrich Schlegel, gives in 1812 a retrospective portrait of Schiller in his classical phase which suggests the opposite:

> What violent transitions do we see in Schiller's mature years! What constant struggle with himself and the world, with the philosophy of the time and with his own art! Restless in himself and ceaselessly tossed about, we also see him totally gripped by the great external convulsion of his age and echoing it in his own emotions. This is why I would like him thought of as a 'revolutionary' poet and it is a quality I find to a greater or lesser extent in all excellent writers of that epoch.[23]

One can find innumerable statements in Schiller which would make the adjective 'revolutionary' quite absurd if applied to him in his mature, classical period. But Schlegel knew Schiller and knew the times and his commentary must be taken seriously. It makes Schiller's declared position one precariously maintained against forces which he knew to be superior and imparts a degree of tension to the aesthetic solutions he offers which is absent from the usual image of Schiller in the scholarly portrayal of Weimar Classicism.

Goethe's response to the Revolution is extremely complex and one cannot dismiss it, as does the eminent critic Hans Mayer, by saying that Goethe simply did not understand.[24] In some ways he understood it too well. Goethe's preferred view of history had no place for apocalyptics. The image of history he liked most was that of the development of each nation as an organic life, imitating the growth of a plant, with certain changes being appropriate to each stage. History should have obeyed the laws of Nature, and so Goethe was inclined to see the French Revolution as a profanation of Nature itself. Like Schiller, he strove to create in his works a vision of humanity in an ideal state of neutrality, purified of the dross of historical accident. In writing of his own modern epic *Hermann und Dorothea*, he says: 'In the crucible of this epic, I have tried to separate the pure humanity of a small German city from its dross and at the same time set out to reflect from a small mirror the great movements and upheavals on the world stage.'[25] As with the supposed presence of the 'monstrous opposition' in *Iphigenie*, it is questionable whether the middle-class idyll of *Hermann und Dorothea* really does give an adequate reflection of such great movements and upheavals. But it is interesting that Goethe feels obliged to have done so, much as the Revolution was to remain for his sensibility the unassimilable *par excellence*. For all his hostility to it, he rarely attempts to disguise the overwhelmingly superior force of History in his non-literary writing. At one point he writes of himself:

> The poet could not go fast enough to catch up with the speed of world events and so could not present either himself or others with an adequate conclusion, seeing as he did the enigma solved once and for all in such a radical and unpredicted manner. . . . But I tried to save myself from these hideous disasters by declaring the whole world to be worth nothing.[26]

However the plays Goethe wrote directly about the Revolution, *Der Bürger-General* and *Die Aufgeregten*, are less than distinguished attempts to trivialize German manifestations of revolutionary spirit through comedy. In his tragedy *Die natürliche Tochter* and his *Wilhelm Meister*, themes pertaining to the Revolution are subtly woven in, but any explicit reckoning with or analysis of the phenomenon is avoided. In a conversation with Eckermann in 1824 he explains his attempt to ridicule revolutionary stirrings in Germany:

> It is true, I could not be a friend of the French Revolution, for its horrors were too close to me and revolted me every day and every hour, whereas its beneficent effects were then not yet visible. Nor could I stand indifferently by when it was attempted in Germany to bring about *artificially* similar scenes to those which in France had been the result of a great necessity.[27]

It is remarkable here that Goethe does seem to have assimilated the purely negative—he can now see benefits and necessities where before he could only see pure destruction. But he is speaking a good twenty years after the high period of Weimar Classicism, and from the insights of his old age he derives scant inspiration for works of a classical temper. If in the works he writes after the outbreak of the Revolution and before Schiller's death there are constant pleas for moderation, for containment within artistic and ethical norms; if the gradual moulding of the individual by a society dominated by the aristocracy is seen most often as man's sovereign good, then we must understand that there is nothing here of the sententious complacency that often accompanies injuctions to do nothing in excess, have one's rough edges rubbed smooth and cultivate the golden mean. Rather there is a constant awareness that his own classical works should, after the manner of the Laocoön or the Rondanini Medusa, assimilate the purely destructive and trans-mute it into beauty, and in this case the purely destructive was history itself. If in Goethe's classical period, such assimilation is more a pious intention than a reality, the works themselves are the more dynamic for it, the familiar attributes of classical style are no less convincing because the final ambition remains unrealized.

I suggest that, in most general terms, the paradoxes and tensions of Weimar Classicism may be understood as emerging from the Enlightenment's failure to achieve clarity as to its own relation to the French Revolution and from the inability of the Romantic epoch in Germany to effect, in the context of real political impotence, a sublimation of the Revolution that did not simul-taneously distort the liberal revolutionary impulse. As a personal amalgam, whose ingredients are selected from a much larger body of European cultural trends, Weimar Classicism does not reflect any confident harmony of experience, but rather acknowledges the pressure to solve problems which its own innate conservatism renders insoluble. If we may speak of a classical temper in such a context, then these factors, together with the very brevity of its realization, exclude any connotations of serenity from the concept. Composure, decorum may be striven for and attained in some works, but these are ultimately emblems of an evanescent synthesis. The potential of failure weighed upon Goethe and Schiller, for they had seen the generation of the Enlightenment fail in its response to the French Revolution, and the threat of failure is often enough to dispel such composure as classical ideals may afford. This is exemplified by a letter from Schiller to the Duke Friedrich Christian von Augustenburg which contains the nucleus of his programme for the aesthetic education of mankind. Writing of the Revolution he says:

Until these events one could succumb to the pleasant delusion that the imperceptible but constant influence of thinking minds, the germs of truth strewn over the centuries, the accumulated treasure of experience—all of these must have made men's hearts more susceptible to the good and thus prepared an epoch in which philosophy could take over the moral framework of the universe and light could conquer darkness. . . . Nothing seemed to be lacking but the signal for a great change—but what has happened! The moment was the most favourable imaginable but it found a corrupt generation of men unworthy of it, unable either to appreciate it or use it.[28]

If this passage begins in the orthodox mode of the Enlightenment and goes on to acknowledge quite in the manner of those anti-classical contemporaries who are usually, though not very accurately, called 'German Jacobins', that the Enlightenment has paved the way for radical social change, the turning at the end displays the German Romantic affection for positing great and simple cosmic movements that are more 'real' than the pragmatics of history and to which one may have recourse when history itself proves too recalcitrant. While the Enlightenment saw mankind as the producer of history, the Romantic view of Germany is by contrast aprioristic, shifting the onus of responsibility from the human sphere to transcendent, impersonal processes. The duty of mankind is no longer to produce, but rather to recognize the pattern and adapt itself to it, and mankind may fail even in this. So, in an unexpected leap, Schiller establishes a benevolent but impersonal force of human history, the fateful Moment, and this has been missed, let down by degenerate mankind. To be forced into such evolutions of double-think, Schiller's initial trauma must have been great, and part of it is clearly the incapacity of a thinker schooled by the Enlightenment to accept its causal nexus with the Revolution. Non-acceptance inevitably enjoins a flight into myth, but not into the mythical harmony of the Classical Age in Greece where both Goethe and Schiller so loved to dwell. Rather the tensions of the situation seem to oblige Schiller to resort to one of the more violent episodes in Christian mythology, an area which the Weimar Classicists preferred to avoid but which was all the more favoured by the German Romantics. And so Schiller, in invoking the myth of the revolt and fall of the angels, must break his classical frame of reference entirely to express the full violence of this contradiction: 'Sensuous man cannot fall further than to the beasts; but if enlightened man falls, then he becomes a fiend and plays a reckless game with the most sacred good of mankind.'[29]

Notes

1. Unless otherwise indicated, Goethe's works and letters are quoted from the Hamburger Ausgabe in 14 vols., ed. E. Trunz *et al.*, Hamburg, 1959, and from *Goethes Briefe*, Hamburger Ausgabe in 4 vols., ed. K. R. Mandelkow, Hamburg, 1962–7. (Abbreviation: HA vii, HAB ii, etc.). Goethe's letter of 20 Dec 1786 to Charlotte von Stein: 'So ist eine Medusenmaske wo in einer hohen, schönen Gesichtsform das ängstliche Starren des Todes unsäglich trefflich ausgedruckt ist' (HAB ii. 32).

2. *Italienische Reise*, April 1788: 'und, um anderes zu übergehen, ein guter alter Abguß der Medusa Rondanini; ein wundersames Werk, das, den Zwiespalt zwischen Tod und Leben, zwischen Schmerz und Wollust ausdrückend, einen unnennbaren Reiz wie irgendein anderes Problem über uns ausübt' (HA xi. 546.).

3. Letter to King Ludwig I of Bavaria of 25 Dec 1825: 'Vor mir aber steht ein langersehntes, einer mythischen Urzeit angehöriges Kunstwerk . . .' (Johann Wolfgang Goethe, *Briefe*, Munich, 1958, p. 993). Cf. Hans Blumenberg, *Arbeit am Mythos*, Frankfurt am Main, 1979, pp. 21 ff.

4. Letter to Zelter of 21 Jan 1826: 'Dieser Anblick, der keineswegs versteinerte, sondern den Kunstsinn höchlich und herrlich belebte, entbehrte ich nun seit vierzig Jahren . . .' (HAB iv. 177).

5. *Über Laokoon* (1797): 'So brachten die Künstler durch Mannigfaltigkeit ein gewisses Gleichgewicht in ihre Arbeit, milderten und erhöhten Wirkung durch Wirkungen und vollendeten sowohl ein geistiges als ein sinnliches Ganzes . . .' (HA xii. 65).

6. Schiller's letter to Körner, 21 Jan 1802 (HA v. 104): 'Sie ist ganz nur sittlich; aber die sinnliche Kraft, das Leben, die Bewegung und alles, was ein Werk zu einem echten dramatischen specificiert, geht ihr sehr ab.'

7. *Italienische Reise*, 19 Oct 1786: 'Der Künstler hat ihr eine gesunde, sichere Jungfräulichkeit gegeben, doch ohne Kälte und Rohheit. Ich habe mir die Gestalt wohl gemerkt und werde ihr im Geist meine "Iphigenie" vorlesen und meine Heldin nichts sagen lassen, was diese Heilige nicht aussprechen möchte' (HA xi. 107).

8. *Dichtung und Wahrheit III, 15*: 'Doch auch die Kühneren jenes Geschlechts, Tantalus, Ixion, Sisyphus, waren meine Heiligen . . .' (HA x. 49 ff.).

9. Quoted by Wilfried Malsch, 'Klassizismus, Klassik und Romantik der Goethezeit', in K. O. Conrady ed., *Deutsche Literatur zur Zeit der Klassik*, Stuttgart, 1977, p. 398: 'Goethe und Schiller führten zu einem Kunstideal zurück, das seit den Griechen niemand mehr als geahnt hatte.'

10. Quoted by Karl Robert Mandelkow, 'Wandlungen des Klassikbildes in Deutschland im Lichte gegenwärtiger Klassikkritik' in

K. O. Conrady ed., *Deutsche Literatur zur Zeit der Klassik*, Stuttgart, 1977, p. 437: 'Und so stehen für uns die Beiden da wie zwei herrliche Bäume, die Wurzeln und Wipfel in einander verflochten haben. Wie zwei hohe Eukalyptusstämme sind sie an die Niederungen unseres Daseins gesetzt, die schädlichen Dünste der Tiefe zu bannen, das Land zu entfiebern und Gesundheit darüber hin zu hauchen.' The passage originally appeared in the *Goethe-Jahrbuch*, xxvi (1905), 20.

11. Schiller's letter to Körner 21 Jan 1802 (HA v. 104): 'Hier wollen wir im nächsten Monat Goethes "Iphigenia" aufs Theater bringen . . .'.

12. In this discussion I am indebted to Gerhard Schulz for permitting me to read and use his still unpublished account of Weimar Classicism, in Gerhard Schulz, *Deutsche Literature im Zeitalter der Französischen Revolution und der Koalitionskriege 1789–1806*, to appear in 1983 with the Beck Verlag, Munich.

13. Cf. 'Klassik' in the *dtv–Lexikon in 20 Bänden*, Wiesbaden, 1978.

14. Jacques Barzun, *Classic, Romantic and Modern*, London, 1961 (2nd edn), p. 243.

15. *Maximen und Reflexionen*: 'Klassisch ist das Gesunde, romantisch das Kranke . . . Das Romantische ist schon in seinen Abgrund verlaufen; das Gräßlichste der neueren Produktionen ist kaum noch gesunkener zu denken.' Nos. 863 and 865 (HA xii. 487).

16. Cf. Richard Friedenthal, *Goethe. Sein Leben und seine Zeit*, dtv-edition, Munich, 1968, 341.

17. *An Goethe als er den Mahomet von Voltaire auf die Bühne brachte:*
Du selbst, der uns von falschem Regelzwange
Zur Wahrheit und Natur zurückgeführt,
Der, in der Wiege schon ein Held, die Schlange
Erstickt, die unsern Genius umschnürt,
Du, den die Kunst, die göttliche, schon lange
Mit ihrer reinen Priesterbinde ziert —
Du opferst auf zertrümmerten Altären
Der Aftermuse, die wir nicht mehr ehren?

18. *Literarischer Sansculottismus*: 'Wann und wo entsteht ein klassischer Nationalautor? Wenn er in der Geschichte seiner Nation große Begebenheiten und ihre Folgen in einer glücklichen und bedeutenden Einheit vorfindet . . .' (HA xii. 241).

19. Karl Marx, *Frühschriften*, ed. S. Landshut, Stuttgart, 1964, 216. Cf. Dieter Borchmeyer, *Höfische Gesellschaft und französische Revolution bei Goethe*, Kronberg, 1977, pp. 250 ff.

20. Adam Bergk, *Bewirkt die Aufklärung Revolutionen?* (1795), quoted in. ed. W. Beutin *et al.*, *Deutsche Literaturgeschichte*, Stuttgart, 1979, p. 135: 'Indem sie nun die Ansichten der Dinge verändern und erweitern und den Menschen die Forderungen, die sie machen *sollen* und *dürfen*, an das Herz legen, bereiten sie notwendigerweise Revolutionen vor . . .'.

21. Letter to Herder of 4 Nov 1795: 'Daher weiß ich für den poetischen

Geist kein Heil, als daß er sich aus dem Gebiet der wirklichen Welt zurückzieht ...' *Schillers Werke*, Nationalausgabe, xxviii (Weimar, 1958), 98.

22. 'Aber je mehr das beschränkte Interesse der Gegenwart die Gemüter in Spannung setzt, einengt und unterjocht ...' *Schillers Werke*, Nationalausgabe, xxii (Weimar, 1958), 106.

23. Friedrich Schlegel, *Kritische Friedrich–Schlegel–Ausgabe*, ed. H. Behler, vi (Munich, 1961), 393 ff.: 'Rastlos in sich und unruhig umhergeschleudert, sehen wir ihn aber auch hier und da von der äußern großen Erschütterung des Zeitalters ganz ergriffen ...'.

24. Hans Mayer, *Goethe*, Frankfurt am Main, 1973, p. 35. Cf. Dieter Brochmeyer, pp. 288 ff.

25. Letter to Johann Heinrich Meyer of 5 Dec 1796: 'Ich habe das reine Menschliche der Existenz einer kleinen deutschen Stadt in dem epischen Tiegel von seinen Schlacken abzuscheiden gesucht ...' (HAB ii. 247).

26. *Campagne in Frankreich:* 'Der Dichter konnte der rollenden Weltgeschichte nicht nacheilen und mußte sich und anderen den Abschluß schuldig bleiben ...' (HA x. 359).

27. 'Es ist wahr, ich konnte kein Freund der Französischen Revolution sein ...' Johann Peter Eckermann, *Gespräche mit Goethe in den letzten Jahren seines Lebens*, ed. Ernst Merian-Genast, Basle, 1945, pp. 514 ff.

28. 'Ehe diese Ereignisse eintraten, Gnädigster Prinz, konnte man sich allenfalls mit dem lieblichen Wahne schmeicheln ...' (letter of 13 July 1793, quoted in *Die Französische Revolution im Spiegel der deutschen Literatur*, ed. Claus Träger, Frankfurt am Main, 1979, pp. 265 ff.).

29. Ibid. pp. 266 ff.: 'Es waren also nicht freie Menschen, die der Staat unterdrückt hatte, nein, es waren bloß wilde Tiere ...'.

8

The Classical Temper in Historiography

Francis West

It is tempting to begin this paper with a paradox. Because there are no classical historians, the classical temper in historiography is of quite peculiar interest. Before the tempers of those who write about the classical past rise in indignant protest, let me resolve the paradox. The classical historians whom I have in mind are not our distinguished contemporaries. Rather are they those who, in classical antiquity itself, wrote about the past of their own societies. Their names are well known: Herodotus, Thucydides, Xenophon, Polybius, Livy, Tacitus, Suetonius and Sallust, to mention only the major ones. These Greek and Roman writers certainly wrote about affairs in the past of their own societies. They did not, however, suppose that their own society had a past which was alien to them, in the sense of being significantly different from their contemporary society, and therefore properly to be studied in its own terms. When, during the Renaissance and still more during the Enlightenment, later European writers came to deal with the past, they too shared that classical attitude. They shared it not simply because they looked back to classical models, or even because, in significant instances, they thought of themselves as Augustans or neoclassicals, but also because their own contemporary circumstances led them to a similar lack of interest in the past in its own terms.

Such an attitude towards the past reflected in the writers of classical antiquity was not the result of any lack of interest in alien societies as such. On the contrary, Greek and Roman writers were ready enough to describe the alien societies of Persia and the East, of Egypt, of Germany and of Britain; yet they looked at the past of their own society not as a remote and alien one but as a projection of their own times or world. The people of Homer or the companions of Aeneas were not alien strangers to the classical writers of later centuries; rather were they contemporaries who simply happened to have lived several centuries earlier. The point has been made in another way by M. I. Finley, who notices the timeless qualities of Greek writing about the past.[1] The reasons for this attitude towards the past in classical antiquity are not the topic of this paper, but one reason must be mentioned because it is different from anything in the situation of Renaissance and Enlightenment writers. The ancient historians (to use the title for the sake of brevity) had neither the necessary materials nor the techniques for historical study of their own past beyond the testimony of their contemporaries. Hecateus of Miletus said: 'The stories of the Greeks are numerous and in my opinion ridiculous.' Thucydides, described by F. M. Cornford as *mythistoricus*, deliberately restricted himself to the history of his own time.[2] It is, too, a commonplace that Livy's books on Roman history come to life only when they deal with his own lifetime.

If, therefore, by the classical temper in historiography is meant the attitude of the writers of classical antiquity towards the past, this comes close to saying that history is the study and narration of the events of one's own life and times, not necessarily as a single point of view, but at least as the view of contemporary testimony. But those who have written about the past, either in the classical past itself or in the belief that they were themselves neoclassical, the heirs of Greece and Rome, have generally meant more than this. They have meant that whether the past about which they wrote was classical or neoclassical, the reason for its study is its relevance to the present. Relevance has become a somewhat discredited word in recent times, but it is an appropriate one to apply to the classical temper in historiography, for if neither the writers of classical antiquity nor those who later imitated them or adapted them had an interest in the past in its own terms, they nevertheless plainly had an interest in its study which came from some contemporary purpose: to provide a model of proper behaviour, to teach practical lessons of statecraft, to find material to use in some contemporary controversy, or simply to contemplate, in some troubled or shadowed present, a vision of perfection, proportion, order and balance.

In antiquity the classical temper towards the past was differently circumstanced from later attitudes in Europe during periods of self-conscious classical revival. To those of the Renaissance, for example, as to those of the Enlightenment who thought of themselves as neoclassical, the survivals of classical antiquity were all around: in buildings, in art, in literature. The classical past was visibly present to the writers of the Renaissance and the Enlightenment as it was not present, as something that had survived, to the ancients themselves.

It was not, however, the only visible past. The medieval (or what came to be called the Gothic) past—the cathedrals, the monasteries, the castles, the manuscripts: these, too, were visibly present, to say nothing of social, legal and political institutions from the Middle Ages. Part of the classical temper, in historiography no less than in architecture, painting and literature, meant the deliberate choice of a classical (not medieval) model. In part that choice was a matter of survivals being newly discovered. There would, I suppose, be few, if any, historians who now hold the simple and unqualified view that the fall of Constantinople and the Roman empire in the east (1453) marked the point at which there was an influx into western Europe of classical texts which had been hitherto unknown or, if known, known only in a poor manuscript tradition. There would, I suppose, be few who would use the term Renaissance without qualification. Nevertheless, whatever date one accepts for the beginning of a Renaissance—whether the revival of interest in, and the study of, humane letters as seen in Petrarch (who died in 1374) or in another Florentine, Bruni (who died in 1444), or in Biondo, a papal official who was writing his *Historiarium ab inclinatione Romanorum imperii decades* between 1440 and 1443—the fact that there *was* a revival of classical antiquity is not in doubt. Yet Bruni and Biondo both wrote their works on the Middle Ages, not on classical Rome; and in doing so they made the division of time which is the very concept of a Middle Age. They did two things. They distinguished the medieval centuries very clearly from classical antiquity, and they distinguished their own age from both. By doing so they made easier the choice of a classical rather than a medieval model.

If there is one word more commonly used than any other of the authors and artists of the Renaissance it is 'humanist': the student of humane letters. Humane letters meant classical letters. It also meant humane as distinct from divine letters, divine being a characterization easily applied to the literature of the Middle Ages. People of the Renaissance knew they belonged to a new age, different from the medieval past. But was it a rebirth of the classical past?

Whatever it may have been for architecture or painting or sculpture, Renaissance historiography neither displayed an interest in classical antiquity for its own sake, nor ignored the Middle Ages which separated that classical past from the present. What it chiefly did was to recover the materials from which the classical past could be reconstructed. By the end of the sixteenth century, all of the major and most of the minor authors of classical antiquity had been printed and published; and classical (not medieval) Latin and Greek had become the basis of a humane education.[3] The primary concern was with the recovery and reconstitution of the classical texts themselves or, more broadly, with the antiquities themselves; and then, as with Scaliger, the reconciliation of the chronology of the classical world with the chronology of the ancient world of the Old Testament. For the Renaissance writers, although they professed humane rather than divine letters, were not pagan classical students. Their humanism, although sceptical of much medieval religion, was nevertheless Christian humanism. Scaliger was an inflexible Protestant humanist. Thomas More was a Catholic humanist. Martin Luther himself said: 'It is a wonderful delight to me to find ... that history and scripture entirely coincide.'[4] The men of the new learning, with their interest in classical survivals, could and did look for human causes of events. They might, in their new age, reject the superstitious or the hagiographical in the Middle Ages; but as with Francis Bacon, who said of Luther that he had had 'to awake all antiquity, and to call former times to his succour ... so that the ancient authors ... which had long time slept in libraries, began generally to be read',[5] they could still believe that there was a divine plan. To discover it, especially if they were also religious reformers who believed that at some point in the past the Catholic church had gone wrong, they were obliged to go back to the Roman past in which the church had, as a matter of history, begun, just as they were obliged, as a matter of theology, to go back to the Greek philosophy of Plato.

The rediscovery of classical antiquity through the texts of its own writers, the increasingly careful reconstitution of those texts, could and did give satisfaction in its own right, just as the study of antiquities, in the words of Lord Halifax in the seventeenth century, '... hath a pleasure in it like that of wrestling with a fine woman'.[6] But there was, for the Reformers who were also Renaissance men, contemporary reason for the study of classical antiquity. Lorenzo Valla's demonstration, on philological grounds, that the Donation of Constantine was a forgery, had a political use against papal claims. Bruni's history of Florence established that the city was founded under the Roman republic, not under the Roman tyranny. There is, of course, nothing distinctive about an interest in the past's being prompted by present political controversies. That, indeed, was why, even if the Renaissance witnessed an attitude of contempt or disdain for the medieval past, it could not nevertheless be ignored, as the argument in England over the 'Ancient Constitution' showed in the seventeenth century.[7] But truth, as some sage has remarked, is independent of the stimulus that provokes it. The stimulus to go back to classical antiquity which the Renaissance represents, although it had an historical aspect, nevertheless did not in fact produce much historiography, while the connected movement of the Reformation stimulated as much interest in the medieval past as in the classical if an answer was to be found to the

Catholic question: where was your church before Luther? The period of religious and political conflicts in the seventeenth century saw men like Mabillon and Montfaucon in France, Spelman and Brady in England, look at the medieval past in its own terms. They were not prompted by the classical models which the textual and philological work of the Renaissance had made both available and familiar to them because of their education. To try to understand the world as it had been was not a lesson they could have learned from the classical authors who were their authorities, for these had never attempted any such thing. Mabillon, in his *De Re Diplomatica*, was answering an unspeakable Jesuit's attack on the charters of the Benedictine Order. Brady, in his history, was disposing of parliamentary myths (as against royalist claims) about an immemorial constitution.[8] Both were engaged in current polemics, but both came to look at the past in its own terms, in a way which makes their work still recognizable by professional historians as the work of peers. Their own contemporaries, and later critics of this kind of history, would have used the word 'antiquarians'.

If these seventeenth-century religious and political conflicts, in Europe and England, focused attention upon the medieval past, the Roman past nevertheless received a share of attention, for the antiquarians—or scholars as, following David Douglas,[9] I should prefer to call them—argued over the Roman or the Germanic, even the Celtic, origins of the medieval institutions they studied. Nevertheless, the classical revival of the Renaissance was chiefly preserved by men of letters, by philologists and by editors of texts, not by those who were historians or antiquarians. And when stability in Church and State returned in the latter part of the seventeenth century to be preserved for most of the eighteenth, the disdain for the Middle Ages then included the work of those who had recently studied it as a matter of some contemporary urgency. The men of the Enlightenment, the neoclassicals or Augustans, could afford to ignore a past which seemed irrelevant to them. Voltaire, for example, standing for the rational humanist, sceptical of any divine plan as the men of the Renaissance had not been, made the point: 'All history is equal for those who wish only to store their memory with facts; but whoever thinks, or, what is more rare, possesses taste, counts only four centuries in the history of mankind.'[10] The centuries were those of Pericles, of the Antonine emperors, of Louis XIV, and Voltaire's own. Edward Gibbon, pre-eminently the historian of the Enlightenment, opened his *Decline and Fall of the Roman Empire* with an even more exclusive view: 'In the second century of the Christian era, the empire of Rome comprehended the fairest part of the earth and the most civilized portion of mankind.' But Gibbon did not share Voltaire's contempt for mere erudition. He had felt obliged, for example, to make himself acquainted with the work of Montfaucon, in whom he recognized 'a taste for true learning'—although he also felt obliged to apologize for his acquaintance with it. It might cause a blush where an acquaintance with the work of the philosopher and mathematician Leibniz would be 'ennobling'.[11]

Gibbon's remark is revealing of the classical temper of the historiography of the Enlightenment, which was more self-consciously classical than that of the Renaissance. His generation were called Augustans and thought of themselves in that way, as their funerary monuments show. It was not simply that in Parliament educated men could correct each other's classical quotations and quantities, nor even that they thought in classical parallels. 'I have heard', said one, talking of the Whig revolution of 1688–9, 'of the geese which saved Rome. I have never heard that the geese were made consuls.' Their education in humane letters led them naturally to think in that way and to see the society in which they lived, and the political institutions within which they worked, as balanced and in proportion. This is most obviously true of such a man as Edmund Burke. 'Our political system is placed in a just correspondence and symmetry with the order of the world, and with the mode of existence decreed to a permanent body composed of transitory parts.'[12] But I doubt if a corresponding Frenchman, in the period from the reign of Louis XIV until the Revolution, would have differed very much about the rightness of the classical proportions of his own institutions, although his classical model (because of the nature of the French monarchy and its location of the sovereign will) might be a different one from the British—the Empire, not the Republic; just as in the numerous, small German states the model of classical antiquity might be different again—the Greek city-state rather than the unitary Roman one.

When these eighteenth-century European heirs of classical antiquity looked at the past, they might indeed take as their model the historians of classical antiquity and so insensibly adopt a similar attitude to the past; but they might also read the classical authors because of the conscious affinities which they felt with them, including their attitude to the past. Bolingbroke, for example, held the view that the past must be relevant to the present. He advised his reader to study carefully the history of the period since the resurrection of letters.[13] To be learned about the Middle Ages was 'a ridiculous affectation in any man who means to be useful to the present age'; 'to be entirely ignorant' would be 'shameful' but there should only be 'a temperate curiosity in the review of them':

> A new system of causes and effects, that subsists in our time, and whereof our conduct is to be a part, arising at the last period [i.e. the

Renaissance], and all that passes in our time being dependent on what has passed since that period, or being immediately relative to it, we are extremely concerned to be well-informed about all these passages.[14]

Bolingbroke's view of the past—that it must be relevant to the present—is natural enough to a practising politician, even an unsuccessful one, but to be useful to present conduct, the past meant the recent past. 'Particular examples may be of use sometimes in particular cases; but the application of them is dangerous. It must be done with the utmost circumspection, or it will be seldom done with success.' Bolingbroke had read the classical authors, just as he had read the Old Testament, and concluded:

> We have therefore neither in profane nor in sacred authors such authentic, clear, distinct, and full accounts of the originals of ancient nations, and of the great events of those ages which are commonly called the first ages, as deserve to go by the name of history, or as afford sufficient materials for chronology and history.[15]

Why then should the remote past be studied at all, if it offers no full account and is therefore of admittedly limited usefulness to conduct in the present time? Bolingbroke answers in a well-known passage:

> We ought always to keep in mind, that history is philosophy teaching by example how to conduct ourselves. . . . [There are] certain general principles, and rules of life and conduct, which always must be true, because they are comfortable to the invariable nature of things. He who studies history as he would study philosophy, will soon distinguish and collect them, and by doing so will form to himself a general system of ethics and politics on the surest foundations, on the trial of these principles and rules in all ages, and on the confirmation of them by universal experience. . . . In this manner the study of history will prepare us for action and observation.[16]

This attitude towards the past uses relevance to present conduct as one criterion, and it also implies that, since there are general and universally true principles, one need gather only the illustrations of them from the past that are sufficient to confirm them. A systematic study of the past is not necessary.

There is an obvious danger in characterizing an historical temper by reference to a few writers, and extracting from them a common denominator which may be misleading if it excludes differences in favour of similarities. There is the further complication that, with writers from different European societies, different social or political factors may produce similar, but not for that reason necessarily related, results. Nevertheless, if the term Enlightenment is a useful one to cover complex phenomena, there is one characteristic which can be taken as a convenient point of reference. Just as Humanism has been used of the Renaissance, so Reason may be used of the Enlightenment. Voltaire, Gibbon and Bolingbroke, for example, had certain things in common. They moved easily in European, as distinct from any national, society. Voltaire knew Bolingbroke and his work, as he later knew Gibbon's.[17] Whatever the differences between them, all regarded themselves as men of Reason. Only Gibbon is commonly called an historian; although Voltaire has sometimes, with more flattery than truth, been claimed as the Father of modern historiography. More usually he and Bolingbroke are called philosophers or political thinkers. They themselves would have accepted 'men of letters'. Nevertheless, Voltaire and Gibbon wrote about the past; Bolingbroke wrote about the use of the study of the past. What had they in common—other than the fact that each of them moved with ease in European society in a self-consciously neoclassical phase?

They shared an assumption that the laws which governed both society and individual behaviour, like the laws of physics and mathematics which governed nature, were rationally derived from natural not divine order. The philosophers and natural philosophers in whose shadow they wrote their history were Descartes and Locke, Newton and Leibniz. Now, Reason and the laws of society which can be derived from it are a-historical, for Reason itself and any such laws are established independently of any historical demonstration based upon past events, and therefore independently of any historical changes. They are, to use Bolingbroke's words, 'general principles . . . which always must be true'. Locke illustrates the point. Although he has often been seen in the context of the argument over sovereign will in seventeenth-century England, and specifically in the context of the Glorious Revolution of 1688–9, his *Two Treatises of Government* are remarkably free from any references to English history, from any appeal to the past.[18] He was certainly aware of some of the work of the protagonists, the antiquarians or scholars who did battle on historical grounds over the king and parliament and the 'immemorial' constitution; but Locke's own argument against sovereign will derives from the principles of nature and reason which lie outside history and which do not change. Historical events are necessary neither to establish the proper polity nor the proper conduct of an individual. They are simply useful illustrations which might, as both Voltaire and Gibbon say, improve the taste and train the intellect; or which might widen—necessarily vicariously, since no one can actually live in the past—the range of individual experience.

To the extent that those who wrote on the past were, as educated men, influenced by such Enlightenment philosophy (and they would have regarded it as shameful not to have at least an acquaintance with it), the historiography of the Enlightenment has an a-historical character. But philosophy was by no means the sole influence which prompted this attitude to the past. If, as a generalization, the eighteenth century was a period of political stability in Europe after the religious wars of the seventeenth and before the outbreak of the revolution towards the close of the eighteenth, and if (as in Britain) this stability came to have a correct symmetry and proportion for many contemporaries besides Burke, it also came to be accepted as an inheritance, handed down and to be preserved, although perhaps with a little alteration to adjust or re-adjust proportion. Given that there was this belief in the correspondence and conformity to nature in the institutions of society, there was little incentive to enquire how it had come about. Because it was conformable to the law of nature, what was important was that, acting always as if in the presence of canonized forefathers who had handed down the inheritance, any action which might upset the balance should be avoided, as indeed it would be if it was 'tempered with an awful gravity'.[19] That is Burke's view of the British Constitution. The 'awful gravity' which thus tempered present action might be achieved by contemplation of the past—to be more precise, of that part of the past which, in a much more remote time, had also achieved classical symmetry and proportion. Gibbon begins his book with the perfection of the Antonine emperors. By showing how Rome declined and fell, he could provide an illustrative and literary account that had lessons to be drawn from it, lessons of a reassuring kind: 'It couldn't happen here and now.' Voltaire had much the same intention when he described a more recent Golden Age, that of Louis XIV. The past was useful to point lessons which would improve the mind, and, in his case, adjust some lack of proportion in the present age of Louis XV, without raising the spectre of a new barbaric age which might succeed the Enlightenment. This classical temper of a present symmetry obviously did not exclude the idea of human progress. Men *had* become more civilized. But how this had happened interested these writers less than how such a civilized classical or neoclassical world might decline and fall.

In selecting those parts of the past which were classical as the proper subject of study—to illustrate general principles which were conformable with the laws of nature, to improve the mind and taste —a great deal of human history was ruled out as unfit for serious study. It was fit only for antiquarians, the merely erudite who wished simply to store their memories with facts; in Bolingbroke's words, 'they deserve encouragement, however, while they continue to compile, and neither affect wit, nor presume to reason'.[20] It was not necessary to be learned about any part of the past that was not useful to the civilized men of the present. This classical temper, however, in selecting classical or neoclassical periods for study, concentrated upon a past which was revealed by literary sources, by classical authors whose works were themselves narratives based on sources which they seldom quoted and still less handled critically, and not upon record or archival material such as the seventeenth-century writers had had access to. Voltaire might use a little archival, as distinct from narrative, material. Gibbon might read Spanheim on ancient medals and Montfaucon on classical archeological materials, but his main sources were the literary narratives of those who in antiquity wrote about its past. What Gibbon achieved, in what his contemporaries commonly regarded as a literary masterpiece, was an elegant synthesis of these narrative writers of classical antiquity. As Adam Smith told him: 'By the universal assent of every man of taste and learning whom I either know or correspond with, the Decline and Fall sets you at the very head of the whole literary tribe at present existing in Europe.' Literary, *not* historical, tribe. Gibbon himself regarded history as a branch of literature and his treatment of his literary sources was not analytical. He might weigh their sometimes conflicting statements and opt for one rather than the other, but his criterion for deciding which was to be preferred derived from those general principles of behaviour which, as Bolingbroke put it, were true at all times. Such were the critical principles of Gibbon's own day, and they are not essentially different from the test which Voltaire said (as distinct from clearly using) he applied—*vraisemblance*.

It was, however, not simply the periods of affinity in the past which were selected for study and elegant narration. Within such a period, some topics were less properly to be dealt with than others. Gibbon, when at the age of twenty-one he wrote an essay in French on the study of literature, was happy to assert:

> Among a multitude of historical facts, there are some, and those by much the majority, which prove nothing more than that they are facts. There are others which may be useful in drawing a partial conclusion, whereby the philosopher may be enabled to judge of the motives of an action, or some particular feature in a character. . . . What is still more rarely to be met with is, a genius who knows how to distinguish them, amid the vast chaos of events . . . and deduce them, pure and unmixt, from the rest.[21]

When he came to write the *Decline and Fall*, he indeed ordered a mass of facts from which a philosopher might draw more than a partial conclusion. 'I have described', he said, 'the triumph of barbarism and religion.'

It was his description of the latter which caused others to object to his ordering of facts. Some wished that he had ignored those aspects which did not bear civilized contemplation: the irrational and superstitious enthusiasms of the early Christians. The more common denunciation came from the theological rancour aroused by his two famous chapters on Christianity at the end of the first volume. Dean Milman of St Paul's characterized the work as 'a bold and disingenuous attack upon Christianity', while one edition was literally bowdlerized, for Thomas Bowdler himself issued it with all the religious material expurgated. Gibbon made only one public answer to his critics. He was reluctant to be drawn into the Deist controversy for which the *Decline and Fall* provided so much material, and he wrote in his *Autobiography* that had he foreseen the effect of those two chapters upon 'the pious, the timid and prudent', he might have been tempted to soften them. When he had originally written them, however, he had regarded them as essential: 'A candid but rational enquiry into the progress and establishment of Christianity may be considered as a very essential part of the history of the Roman empire.'[22] He had nevertheless almost immediately added:

> The scanty and suspicious materials of ecclesiastical history seldom enable us to dispel the dark cloud that hangs over the first age of the church. ... The theologian may indulge the pleasing task of describing Religion as she descended from Heaven, arrayed in her native purity. A more melancholy duty is imposed on the historian. He must discover the inevitable mixture of error and corruption which she contracted in a long residence upon earth.

The scepticism is clearly implied, as indeed it was in other phraseology, such as his description of Saint Simeon Stylites' pillar as his 'last and lofty station'.[23] The orthodox Christians drew the inference. But to rational, civilized men of the Enlightenment the lesson was also clear. The decline of Rome, said Gibbon,

> was the natural and inevitable effect of immoderate greatness. Prosperity ripened the principle of decay; the causes of destruction multiplied with the extent of conquest; and as soon as time or accident had removed the artificial supports, the stupendous fabric yielded to the pressure of its own weight. The story of its ruin is simple and obvious, and instead of inquiring why the Roman empire was destroyed, we should rather be surprised that it had subsisted so long. ... The victorious legions who in distant places acquired the vices of strangers and mercenaries first oppressed the freedom of the

republic and afterwards violated the majesty of the purple ... the
vigour of military government was relaxed and finally dissolved by
the partial institutions of Constantine; and the Roman world was
overwhelmed by a deluge of barbarians.[24]

This 'awful revolution', concludes Gibbon, 'may be usefully applied
to the instruction of the present age.' These remote events could not
essentially injure the present general state of happiness, the system
of arts and law and manners 'which so advantageously distinguish,
above the rest of mankind, the Europeans and their colonies'. The
savage nations of the globe were still the common enemies of civilized society, but in his own day, explains Gibbon, with science
applied to the art of war, Europe is secure from barbarism since,
before they can conquer, the barbarians must cease to be
barbarians.

This complacency in Gibbon assumes that the present general
state of happiness—of order and of moderation, of due proportion
in state and church—makes the past irrelevant to the lives of the
present. Security, in short, loosened the ties which bound men to the
past. What had happened in the past could not vitally affect the
present whose happiness came from general principles independent
of historical events in the past. Why then study it at all? Bolingbroke, Voltaire and Gibbon, to say nothing of the professors of
Göttingen and Edinburgh,[25] returned the same answer: to inculcate
the practical and moral lessons useful to men of affairs, to furnish
examples for philosophical reflection, to cultivate the mind and
improve taste. To do any of these things, the form and style of the
accounts they offered were as important as the content. The formal
aspects of their writing, with the balanced prose periods, like the
Alexandrine or the heroic couplet in verse, reflected the order and
symmetry appropriate to both their themes and the classical literary
sources they used. It was possible for Gibbon, or any other
contemporary writer on classical antiquity, to know the whole of the
surviving literature upon which they relied for their description of
the classical past; and to see the task not as the critical analysis of
these relatively scanty materials but as their synthesis or
concordance into an elegant narrative. As Lytton Strachey wrote of
Gibbon: 'He drove a straight, firm road through the vast unexplored
forest of Roman history; his readers could follow with easy pleasure
along the wonderful way ... but they were not invited to stop, or
wander, or camp out, or make friends with the natives.'[26]

If the consequence of this classical temper in writing about the
past was to produce a literary narrative of use, even if only as polite
letters for the pleasure of leisured and contemplative reading
(although the authors intended its more serious and philosophical

use), it is scarcely surprising that it has left little that is now useful to professional historians of the same period. In this there is a contrast with seventeenth-century scholarship, which is still of professional importance. Nevertheless the classical temper contributed something that was missing from that earlier historiography. If the classical temper showed little concern with the past in its own terms, and little concern with how classical or neoclassical order and proportion came into existence, its concern with possible decline and fall at least obliged its authors to take account of change in human affairs. Where the Renaissance humanists might still invoke a divine providence, the Enlightenment rationalists sought their causation in human nature. Where the seventeenth-century scholars showed little concern with or ability to explain how one age changed into another, Voltaire, for example, and Gibbon both regarded the accounts which they themselves wrote not simply as literature or polite letters but as an account of cause and effect. Their type of causation may be different from that which any modern historian would normally give similar weight to (although it has been claimed for Voltaire that he founded social and economic history).[27] But in looking for causes they were clearly accepting the concept of change in response to rational human perceptions of circumstances, and were interested in formulating laws by which change occurred.

And in this, to end as I began, there is a paradox. If the classical temper of eighteenth-century historiography—by contrast with the temper of the seventeenth-century scholars who could not account for change, with the Renaissance men of humane letters who could still invoke a Divine Plan or Providence, and with the writers of classical antiquity who assumed a timeless and therefore contemporary past—recognized the fact of change and endeavoured to explain it, nevertheless change, in any fundamental sense, lay in the past. It had obviously occurred in the decline and fall of earlier classical perfection, but it did not threaten the present classical symmetry. Change, in the classical temper, came to a full stop. In this it differs from the usual concept of progress, but it has a good deal in common with those whose conception of time ends with the idea of Heaven.

Notes

1. *The Use and Abuse of History*, London, 1973, p. 16.
2. F. M. Cornford, *Thucydides Mythistoricus*, London, 1907. A. W. Verrall, writing to Cornford on 5 March 1907, said: 'I cordially

welcome your demolition of the exaggerated view that Thucydides fully developed what we call the scientific view of human life and history', quoted in R. Ackerman, 'Some Letters of the Cambridge Ritualists', *Greek, Roman and Byzantine Studies*, xii (no. 1), 120.

3. R. Pfeiffer, *History of Classical Scholarship*, Oxford, 1974. See also G. N. Clark, *The Seventeenth Century*, Oxford, 1950 (2nd edn), p. 270; E. Fueter, *Geschichte des neueren Historiographie*, Berlin, 1936; L. Traube, *Vorlesungen und Abhandlung zur Päleographie und Handschriftenkunde*, Munich, 1909.

4. Luther's preface to *Vitae Romanorum pontificum* (1535).

5. *The Advancement of Learning*, I. iv. 2.

6. *The Complete Works of George Savile, First Marquis of Halifax*, ed. Walter Raleigh, Oxford, 1912, p. 249.

7. J. G. A. Pocock, *The Ancient Constitution and the Feudal Law*, Cambridge, 1957, pp. 1–2.

8. Ibid. pp. 182–228.

9. D. C. Douglas, *The English Scholars*, London, 1943.

10. *Le Siècle de Louis XIV*, in *Œuvres Complètes*, ed. L. Moland, Paris, 1877–85, xiv. 55.

11. J. W. Swain, *Edward Gibbon the Historian*, London, 1966, p. 141.

12. *Reflections on the Revolution in France*, ed. William B. Todd, New York, 1965 (3rd printing), p. 38.

13. *The Works of Lord Bolingbroke*, Philadelphia, 1841, ii. 238ff.

14. Ibid. ii. 239.

15. Ibid. ii. 191, 211.

16. Ibid. ii. 191, 193, 194.

17. J. H. Brumfitt, *Voltaire: Historian*, Oxford, 1958, pp. 40–5.

18. Pocock, pp. 237–8.

19. *Reflections on the Revolution in France*, p. 39.

20. Works, ii. 174.

21. *Essai sur l'étude de la littérature*, London, 1761, sect. XLIX (quoted from the 'first' English translation, London, 1764, pp. 99–100).

22. *Decline and Fall*, ch. 15.

23. Ibid. ch. 37.

24. Ibid. ch. 38.

25. D. Forbes, 'Historismus in England', *Cambridge Journal*, April 1951, pp. 389–90.

26. *Portraits in Miniature and Other Essays*, London, 1931, pp. 161–2.

27. Brumfitt, p. 207. This claim is not borne out by Voltaire's historical work. It might better be made for Robertson; cf. Pocock, pp. 273ff.

Index